Arts and Crafts of Mexico

CHLOË SAYER

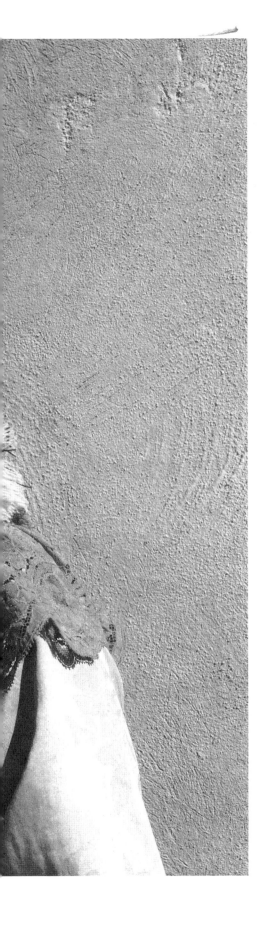

ARTS AND CRAFTS OF MEXICO

With 213 illustrations, 160 in colour

Special photography by David Lavender

THAMES AND HUDSON

AUTHOR'S NOTE

This book is affectionately dedicated to Ruth D. Lechuga and Mariana Yampolsky, whose vast knowledge has been generously shared over many years. Their enthusiasm for the arts and crafts of Mexico has been a great source of inspiration.

Much of the information contained in this book was gained on field trips to Mexico with Elizabeth Carmichael, friend and travelling companion. I should like to thank the Trustees of the British Museum for permission to photograph objects from the collections; I am indebted to Helen Wolfe and Jim Hamill for their kindness during photographic sessions, and to Andrew Cockrill for the loan of photographic equipment.

This book could not exist without the creativity and ingenuity of Mexico's countless craftworkers. Special mention must go to Ana Cecilia Cruz Alberto, Guadalupe Panduro, Efrain Martínez Zuluaga, Fidel Navarro, Roberto Ruiz, Faustina Sumano de Sánchez, Julio Angel Valera and Aarón Velasco Pacheco, who demonstrated their skills in London in 1981 and whose work appears here. It also gives me enormous pleasure to include work by the Linares family, Fredy Mendez, Crispina Navarro Gómez, Tiburcio Soteno and Maurilio Rojas. This book is a tribute to the artisans listed above, and to the many whose work appears but whose names I have been unable to discover. My deepest thanks are due to David Lavender, whose photographs so beautifully convey the richness of Mexico's craft heritage.

PREVIOUS PAGE *Mazahua woman from San Simón de la Laguna in the State of Mexico wearing a profusion of inexpensive adornments.*

© 1990 Thames and Hudson Ltd, London

Printed and bound in Singapore

CONTENTS

CHAPTER I

INTRODUCTION

'I HAVE SEEN THE THINGS which were brought to the King from the new golden land ... a sun all of gold ... and a moon all of silver ... wondrous weapons ... strange clothing ... and all manner of marvellous things for many uses .... In all the days of my life I have seen nothing that so rejoiced my heart as these things, for I saw among them wonderful works of art, and I marvelled at the subtle genius of men in distant lands.'

These words were written in 1520 by the great German artist, Albrecht Dürer. The 'new golden land' was Mexico; the 'works of art' had been given by the Aztec emperor Moctezuma to Hernán Cortés and sent by sea to Charles V, the King of Spain and recently elected Holy Roman Emperor. Although such treasures represented some of the highest technological achievements of the New World, their arrival in Europe also heralded the overthrow of their Indian creators. When Cortés landed at Veracruz with just four hundred fellow Spaniards, the Aztec dominated most of central Mexico. In two years they and their allies faced defeat, and the Conquest of Mexico was secured for Spain.

Cortés and his followers have left us descriptions of the Aztec capital and its market, where richly patterned textiles, feathers, gourds and precious metals were sold in abundance. Because their civilization evolved late in pre-Conquest history, the Aztec were able to adopt the craft skills and cultural traits of many other peoples such as the Toltec, the Mixtec, the Zapotec and the Maya. Under Spanish rule some indigenous crafts disappeared, but others were introduced from Europe and taught in mission schools. In 1565 the Philippines came under Spanish domination, and shipments of exotic merchandise from the Orient offered further inspiration to the craftsmen and -women of Mexico.

Independence from Spain was won in 1821. For the next ninety years, periods of turmoil and economic crisis alternated with stretches of political stability. Then, with the Revolution of 1910, a new attempt was made to redress the social balance and to bridge the chasm between rich and poor. The 1920s and 30s have often been described as Mexico's Renaissance. Over the centuries intermarriage between Spaniards and Indians had created a vast *mestizo* class. As a wave of nationalism swept the country, Mexico's *mestizos* found a pride in their heritage; painters such as Diego Rivera, Frida Kahlo and Dr Atl helped set a new value on Mexico's past, traditions and folk arts, which had for so long been viewed as inferior to European culture.

Today, more than four-and-a-half centuries after the Conquest, nearly sixty Indian peoples still live in Mexico. It is hard to obtain reliable census figures in the harsh and isolated regions where many groups live, but the Indian popula-

Three Generations. *This photograph shows a Nahua wedding group in Altepexi, Puebla. Although the older woman retains her Indian clothing, younger members of the family are dressed in Western styles.*

LEFT *Mazahua church decoration in the State of Mexico. The Virgin Mary and the infant Jesus are embellished with threaded popcorn and roses.* BELOW *The theme of death inspires many craftworkers, who share the humorous vision expressed by Manuel Manilla during the late nineteenth century. In his engravings, skulls and skeletons are used with irony to show the absurdity of the human condition.*

tion is currently estimated at around 12 million, or 15 per cent of the total. Mexico's widely varying geography provides a range of raw materials for house-building and for the creation of clothing, pots, baskets and other objects necessary for survival. Today the descendants of the Aztec and the Maya no longer build pyramids or paint codices, but the motifs on a water jar or the woven designs of a blanket provide continuity with the past.

In less remote areas Indian and *mestizo* craftsmen build on existing traditions to create objects for sale to tourists and collectors. No longer strictly functional are the wall hangings exuberantly embroidered in Tenango de Doria and, more recently, San Pablito, or the gigantic painted candlesticks incorporating mermaids, birds and animals which have brought fame to potters in Metepec.

Crafts in Mexico remain an essential part of life. They are found more often in markets than in galleries; they are a living tradition, not a nostalgic evocation of a vanished past. Enriched by the fusion of Old and New World materials, forms and techniques, Mexican crafts are at the forefront of popular culture.

The Catholic Church is a rich source of imagery, and devotion to the Virgin of Guadalupe (the patron saint of Mexico) is given a visual form by countless craftworkers (pls 22, 35, 83). Another recurring element is the national emblem, which shows an eagle perched on a prickly pear with a serpent in its beak; this symbol recalls the founding of the Aztec capital (pls 52, 95). Ancient history is often conjured up through carved masks and other crafts (pls 89, 153).

A fascination with death is expressed in many ways (pls 11, 103–5, 108–9, 135–41). As the poet Octavio Paz wrote in *The Labyrinth of Solitude*, 'the Mexican is familiar with death, jokes about it, caresses it, sleeps with it, celebrates it; it is one of his favourite toys and his most steadfast love'. According to popular belief, the departed return to earth each year for the Festival of the Dead. Crafts inspired by this and other celebrations have a spiritual dimension rarely found in the modern world.

1 *Figures of painted tin made by Aarón Velasco Pacheco of Oaxaca city. Average H of figures 4⅛" (10.5 cm).*

2 Miniaturized scene: skeleton gamblers of painted clay play cards in a wooden room. Box (front view) 2¾" x 4¾" (7 x 12 cm).

3 Wooden tile with reptiles made by the Huichol Indians of Jalisco. Glass beads have been pressed down one by one on to the wax-covered surface. 7⅞" x 6½" (20 x 16.5 cm).

4 *Repoussé earrings of silver, shaped like mermaids and inset with stones. Palmillas, State of Mexico. With earpiece L 2⅛" (5.5 cm).*

5 *Sugar fish in a basket made by nuns in Xalapa, Veracruz. L of basket 7¼" (18.5 cm).*

7 *Huichol man's shoulder-bag of factory cloth, embroidered in cross stitch with commercial cotton thread, from San Andrés Cohamiata, Jalisco. 7⅞" sq. (20 cm sq.).*

6 *Ornamental devil mask of lacquered wood with real horns and teeth. Inspired by masks used during the* Pastorela, *or Christmas dance-drama, it was carved by Victoriano Salgado of Uruapan in the State of Michoacán. H (not including horns) 7⅞" (20 cm).*

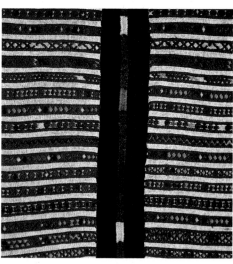

8 *Section of a brocade-patterned* servilleta *(cloth) from San Andrés Chicahuaxtla, Oaxaca. Woven by Esther Sandoval on a backstrap loom with cotton and acrylic yarn, it features an indigo-dyed warp stripe. Area shown 25" sq. (63.5 cm sq.).*

9 *Tiger mask of papier mâché with real whiskers. Until recently such masks were rented out to children in Chilapa, Guerrero. H 10″ (25.5 cm).*

10 *Necklaces of painted clay by Higinio López of Amozoc, Puebla. W shown 10⅝″ (27 cm).*

12 Huichol man's shoulder-bag from Jalisco, double-woven on a backstrap loom from re-spun acrylic yarns. 8″ x 8¾″ (20.2 x 22.2 cm).

11 Beads of rock crystal, carved in the shape of skulls and shells, from Iguala, Guerrero. L of shells approx. 2⅛″ (5.5 cm). H of skulls approx. ¾″ (2 cm).

13 Burnished pot with a reddish slip from the Mixtec village of Pinotepa de Don Luis, Oaxaca. Painted designs include a scorpion. H 12″ (30.5 cm).

14 *Hand-modelled clay animals from Ocotlán, Oaxaca. H of tallest animal 9¼" (23.5 cm).*

15 *Mould- and hand-fashioned clay scene with devils and a dead man, decorated with commercial paints and varnished. From the workshop of Heriberto Castillo in Izúcar de Matamoros, Puebla. H 4¾" (12 cm).*

CHAPTER II

THE TEXTILE ARTS

TEXTILE SKILLS IN MEXICO centre chiefly on the creation of clothing. Throughout its long history Mexican costume has evolved ceaselessly, absorbing new features yet retaining many elements of pre-Hispanic dress. Contemporary textiles derive their richness and variety from the fusion, over many centuries, of different materials, techniques, garment styles and decorative motifs.

Unfortunately for the study of early Mexican costume, few pre-Hispanic textiles survive. Occasional vestiges, preserved most often in dry caves, do however hint at the range of fibres and techniques used, and help archaeologists to chart the advance of textile skills. Despite various theories which suggest that loom weaving was introduced into Mexico from South America, it nevertheless seems probable that weaving evolved independently, inspired by mat-making and similar basketry methods. These techniques, together with netting and twining, were current in central Mexico by 5000 BC, but the oldest loom-woven fragment so far excavated, from south-western Tamaulipas, has been dated to between 1800 and 1400 BC.

To compensate for the shortage of early textiles, pre-Conquest clothing is evoked by a multitude of clay figurines and stone carvings, while polychrome pottery vessels, mural paintings and codices offer further representations. In addition to these visual resources, there are many references to native dress in Spanish records of the Conquest period. Hernán Cortés, in a report to the King of Spain, marvelled at the artistry of dyers and weavers. 'Moctezuma gave me a large quantity of his own textiles', he wrote, 'which, considering they were cotton and not silk, were such that there could not be fashioned or woven anything similar in the whole world for the variety and naturalness of the colours and for the handiwork.'

Although these words describe achievements within the Aztec empire, the textile arts were practised with equal ingenuity in other regions by the Mixtec, the Maya and many other peoples. The exclusive domain of women, skills such as spinning and weaving were usual at every level of society. Each year vast quantities of textiles were offered to the gods; hangings were needed for the inner chambers of temples, and draperies displayed during religious processions. Weavings also served as dowry payments, for marriage ceremonies and as wrappings for the dead, yet it was the creation of clothing that demanded most time and energy. Often costume played a more than functional role. Within Aztec society, which had become highly stratified by the time of the Conquest, dress served to reinforce status through a rigid series of rulings. All but the noble and privileged were barred, sometimes on pain of death, from wearing cotton

16 *Detail of a Nahua woman's wrap-around skirt from Acatlán, Guerrero. Woven on a backstrap loom in two webs from indigo-dyed cotton, it was embroidered with synthetic silk thread using satin and couching techniques. Area shown 42½" x 39⅜" (108 x 100 cm).*

clothing or from adopting certain adornments. This accorded well with Aztec faith in predestination; accustomed to searching for signs and symbols, they vested all things – even a feather or a jewel – with an inner meaning.

Many beliefs and rituals were associated with the textile arts in ancient Mexico. According to the Spanish chronicler Motolinía, it was customary soon after the birth of a baby girl to place in her hand 'a spindle and weaving stick, as a sign that she should be diligent and housewifely, a good spinner and a better weaver'. Maya women sought the protection of Ixchel, goddess of weaving, childbirth, floods and the moon, while among the Aztec the invention of spinning and weaving was attributed to Xochiquetzal, goddess of flowers and patroness of craftworkers. Each year, during the feast of Xochiquetzal, women were burnt in her honour. First, however, sacrificial victims would burn their spinning and weaving equipment, certain that it would await them in the next world.

After the Conquest the introduction of Christianity and the abolition of the old social hierarchy had far-reaching effects on native dress. The noble and ceremonial status of certain garments was eroded. Friars and governors, determined to eradicate cultural traits that they considered 'uncivilized' or 'pagan', outlawed forms of personal adornment such as face and body painting; they also discouraged scanty or 'immodest' dressing. European textile technology was taught in mission centres, and Indian men were initiated into the art of treadle-loom weaving. The Spanish élite, meanwhile, followed European fashions and dressed with splendour. The caste system, maintained throughout the Colonial period, was for a time strengthened by a series of rulings on dress: non-Indians, for example, were barred from using Indian costume styles. Cloth supplies, imported from Spain and after 1565 from the Philippines and China, were supplemented by weavings from Indian looms and from textile factories which grew up in towns.

With Mexican independence in the nineteenth century came the rise of the national textile industry. Synthetic dyes were imported from Europe and new technology was introduced. Sales of factory cloth and later of ready-made garments increased steadily, but in rural areas many traditional techniques persisted. Today, more than four-and-a-half centuries after the Conquest, most Indian peoples retain a particular style of dress, with variations to distinguish different villages within a community. Elaborately woven or embroidered clothing is worn not just on ceremonial occasions but throughout daily life.

Women's costumes reflect the greatest continuity with pre-Hispanic styles. In isolated regions the garments worn by many Mixtec, Maya or Otomí women differ little in form from those of their ancestors. Wrap-around skirts, held in place by waist-sashes, are still widely used. Some are rectangular, but others are seamed to form a tube. Each morning the wearer arranges the skirt anew, creating a series of voluminous folds or tight pleats, according to local custom.

Pottery figurine of the Late Classic period from Jaina, showing a Maya woman wearing a wrap-around skirt under a lozenge-patterned huipil, *or tunic. Similar designs are found today in the highlands of Chiapas (pls 18, 19). H 7½" (19 cm)*

Sashes are prized for their utility and decorative value. They are even thought in some communities to play a medical role: binding, especially during pregnancy, is believed to give valuable support to the stomach.

Also of pre-Hispanic origin is the *huipil*, or sleeveless tunic, which today occurs chiefly in parts of Morelos, Michoacán, Guerrero, Oaxaca, Chiapas and the Yucatán Peninsula. Patterning, construction methods and styles of wearing vary widely. Short examples may be tucked inside the skirt, but longer ones hang freely, often concealing the skirt altogether. Before the Conquest the *huipil* coexisted in some regions with the *quechquemitl*, or closed shoulder-cape. In contemporary Mexico, however, the two garments hardly ever coincide. The *quechquemitl*, which evolved over fifteen centuries ago, is currently worn in many central and northern areas by the Huichol, the Huastec, the Mazahua, the Tepehua, the Totonac, the Otomí and the Nahua, who together employ a remarkable range of decorative techniques.

Quechquemitl are smaller than they once were, perhaps because women are unwilling to cover the increasingly ornate blouses which now accompany them. Introduced after the Conquest by missionaries who found the *quechquemitl* too revealing when worn on its own, the blouse has proved to be Spain's most significant contribution to female dress. Indian ingenuity has devised numerous styles of embellishment. As a result the blouse is gaining popularity in *huipil* regions, replacing this ancient garment altogether in some villages; alternatively *huipiles* may be given sleeve-like trimmings to emulate the blouse (pl. 31). Other European garments to have found favour in Indian Mexico are skirts on waistbands and aprons.

Female costume includes a variety of coverings and head-dresses. In many regions woven textiles serve as capes but are also used to carry loads and babies. In strong sunlight heads may be covered with folded cloths, a second *quechquemitl* or even a palm hat. The most popular protective garment of all, however, remains the *rebozo*, or rectangular shawl. Doubling when necessary as a carrying cloth, the *rebozo* is thought to have originated during the sixteenth century. By the end of the nineteenth century it had become a symbol of Mexican womanhood, depicted in countless *costumbrista* paintings and lithographs. Throughout modern Mexico different styles, often with opulent fringes, are sold in markets and are sometimes worn by *mestizo* as well as Indian women.

Male native dress has undergone more changes since the Spanish Conquest than female dress. Indian men habitually travel further from their villages than women, and their clothing is often shop-bought and indistinguishable from that of non-Indians. In recent decades several fine costumes have died out, but a few groups still adhere to more traditional clothing styles. In Chiapas, for example, some Lacandón men still wear *huipil*-like tunics of cotton cloth, while the Tarahumara of Chihuahua frequently use cotton loincloths during hot weather

Xochiquetzal ('Flower Bird'), the Aztec goddess of flowers and growth, was also the patroness of weavers.

LEFT *Tzeltal dignitaries in Tenejapa, Chiapas. Their* calzones, *or drawers, are barely visible beneath their woollen tunics. They wear necklaces of office, hung with coins and a cross.*
RIGHT *Aztec women from the Codex Florentino with* huipiles *and wrap-around skirts. Such garments are still worn in many areas of Indian Mexico.*

ABOVE *Mixtec priestess from the Codex Zouche wearing a triangular* quechquemitl. *Although no longer a symbol of power and status as it was in pre-Hispanic times, the* quechquemitl *is still worn in many Indian communities.*

with just a woollen sash for support. Widely worn before the Conquest, woven sashes still play an important role in modern Mexico and feature a variety of motifs, despite the spread of leather and plastic belts from factories. Occasionally sash ends are tucked in; more usually, however, they are allowed to hang down. Dimensions differ, but the longest sash in use today, from Huistán in Chiapas, measures an astonishing 15 feet (4.6 metres).

Missionary zeal during Colonial times was responsible for the introduction of shirts and trousers. Interpreted in a number of ways by Indian communities, both garments are generally loose-fitting and constructed without the aid of zips or buttons. Distinctive and often highly decorated examples are found chiefly in the Chiapas highlands, in parts of Oaxaca and among the Huichol, but simpler unadorned versions are worn in many parts of Mexico. To make up for the lack of pockets in Indian dress, most men carry their belongings in shoulder-bags.

During cold weather Indians and some *mestizos* wear a woollen *sarape*, or blanket, with an opening for the head. The counterpart of the *rebozo*, which also evolved under Spanish rule, the *sarape* became during the nineteenth century a symbol of Mexican identity and a focus for masculine pride. Wealthy men could afford veritable works of art incorporating silk and metallic thread. Modern examples are less sumptuous and face competition from mass-produced acrylic replicas, but finely patterned *sarapes* are still woven in a number of regions. Alternatively, sleeveless woollen jackets may be worn in central Mexico, while thick woollen tunics with sleeves are favoured in parts of the Chiapas highlands.

The raw materials and techniques required to make these different garments originate, as do the garments themselves, in both the Old and New Worlds. Mexico's varied geography and climate foster a wide range of trees, shrubs and plants, many of which continue as in pre-Conquest times to provide the elements for clothing. The manufacture of bark cloth has a long history in Mexico. Today it survives among the Lacandón of Lake Najá in Chiapas, where the forests are rich in wild fig-trees. By splitting the bark to the wood the Lacandón are able to tear off long strips. After immersion in water these are beaten with a wooden mallet until the fibres unite and stretch, often to double their original size. Bark-cloth tunics were worn until recently by Lacandón men during non-Christian rituals; now they are sold to collectors and museums, although red-dyed headbands of bark cloth are still offered to the Lacandón gods, who are represented by clay censers with heads.

With few exceptions, however, most articles of dress depend today on loom weaving. The Mexican agave, which includes some two hundred species, remains an important source in many parts of the country for strong and flexible thread. *Agave zapupe* is used by the Huastec Indians of Veracruz, who strip the leaves of pulp by pulling them between two sticks; the smooth white fibres are left to dry and are occasionally dyed before being woven into durable shoulder-bags. The Otomí who inhabit the Mezquital Valley of Hidalgo employ a different method. In this arid and inhospitable region the spikes of local agave plants are severed, baked until soft and left in water to rot; they are then beaten with a mallet, spread across an inclined board and scraped with a metal blade. When the fibres are free of pulp they are soaked in water with a stiffening agent such as maize dough, dried in the sun, combed, spun, and woven into capes.

Cotton is suitable for most types of garment and is more widely used than all other textile yarns. Weavers work as they did before the Conquest with white cotton (*Gossypium hirsutum*) and, in some areas, with a toffee-coloured strain known popularly as *coyuche* (*Gossypium mexicanum*). Among Indians cotton growing has remained a marginal pursuit, quite divorced from the high production levels of industry, which in any case has shown no interest in cultivating *coyuche*. Preparation methods for both types of cotton are long and laborious. First the fibres are separated from the seed pods by hand and freed from impurities. Then the cotton is fluffed out, spread on a thick blanket or palm mat, and beaten with two wooden sticks. Lastly it must be shaped into a smooth strip and rolled in a ball, ready for spinning.

In pre-Hispanic Mexico cotton was interspun for added warmth with downy feathers or with fur from the soft underbelly of rabbits and hares. This custom was superseded by the arrival of wool. Introduced into Mexico by Spanish settlers in the sixteenth century, wool has gained wide acceptance, especially in cold and mountainous areas. In Indian communities it is washed, sometimes with a special soap made from local plants, and carded as in Europe with two boards inset with wire bristles. Many weavers rely on combinations of black, brown, grey and white wool to pattern cloth.

Silk cultivation, established during the early years of Colonial rule, was also successful until banned by a royal decree protecting Spain's own silk industry. Small-scale production continued in remote areas, but was again threatened in the 1930s when widespread spraying against malaria killed off large numbers of silkworm. Fortunately, enough insects and mulberry trees remain in the mountains of Oaxaca to provide Mixtec weavers in a few communities with a regular, if small, supply of silk. Boiled in water with ashes the cocoons turn from yellow to white; once dry, they can be pulled apart. When the Spaniards introduced the domesticated Asiatic silkworm, *Bombyx mori*, into Mexico, they believed – perhaps wrongly – that they were introducing silk itself. Other types of moth also yield silk filaments, however. Today wild silk is woven, as it may have been before the Conquest, by a few women in the highlands of Oaxaca and Puebla.

Methods and implements for spinning these different fibres range from the European to the indigenous. In treadle-loom workshops, where wool is needed in large quantities, the spinning wheel is commonly used, but in most Indian communities spinning is done in pre-Hispanic fashion with the aid of a spindle. The wooden shaft is weighted with a whorl of clay or, less usually, wood, although resourceful Huichol spinners have been known to make whorls from sections of gourd, bone and even broken china. The quality and texture of home-woven cloth are largely determined at this stage: yarn should be smoothly spun and extremely resistant. Spinners sit on a low chair or kneel on a palm mat; while the left hand feeds the fibres on to the tip of the spindle, the right hand keeps it rotating on smooth ground or in a dish. Otomí spinners of agave fibre in the Mezquital Valley follow a different procedure, however. Arrow-shaped at the top end, their spindles are designed to rotate in the air. As a result spinners can work while walking to market or tending their sheep and goats.

Before the Conquest, legend spoke of a marvellous age, during the reign of the Toltec ruler Quetzalcóatl, when cotton grew in many colours. By using a wide range of dyes, weavers are able to restore some of these mythical shades to their yarn. Synthetic colourants have become increasingly popular, but natural dyes from vegetable, mineral and animal sources are still preferred in many villages. Although some are substantive and stain fibres directly, others require mordants to fix them. Ingredients are rarely measured, as weavers work mostly by guesswork. Considerable skill, hard work and patience are required, with operations taking several hours or even several days.

Mixtec spinner from the Codex Vindobonensis. Today many Indian women still spin their thread in pre-Conquest fashion with a spindle. Spun yarns range from the very coarse to the very fine; it might take a weaver approximately three days to turn two pounds of wool into thick thread, but up to two weeks to spin fine thread from the same amount of wool.

Fruits, flowers, leaves, barks and woods all serve as regional dyes. Rich blue-black tones are created with indigo (*Indigofera anil*), and shades of tan and red with brazil-wood (*Haematoxylon brasiletto*) or logwood (*Haematoxylon campechianum*). Lichens mixed with alum provide the Tarahumara with rusty yellow, while in the Chiapas highlands *muicle* (*Jacobinia spicigera*) is mordanted with lime, alum and chrome to give grey with purplish-blue overtones. Other colourants include the seeds of annatto (*Bixa orellana*), which stain a rusty orange, blackberries, which are a source of purple, camomile leaves, which give greenish gold, and countless other plants which go by local names and meet local needs. Inorganic substances, usually found in natural deposits, play a vital role in many dying processes. Mordants such as alum have already been mentioned. Iron oxide, gypsum and ochres furnish stable pigments when mixed with other elements, while in some *rebozo*-weaving centres old iron, left to decompose in water, provides the basis for a strong-smelling black dye.

Two animal colourants, greatly valued before and after the Conquest, persist today despite increasing rarity and rising prices. When Mexico was a Spanish colony, shipments of cochineal to Europe ranked second only to those of precious metals. Today production continues on a small scale and is centred chiefly in Oaxaca. The domesticated cochineal insect, *Dactylopius coccus*, feeds on host cacti of the *Opuntia* or *Nopalea* genus. Wool and silk are both extremely receptive to this dye. Insects may be sun-dried or toasted on griddles, before being ground to powder and mordanted with alum, lime juice or salt. Using different procedures, dyers can achieve not just red and pink, but also near-black and purple shades.

In Mixtec villages such as Pinotepa de Don Luis, striped wrap-around skirts are woven from cochineal-dyed silk and indigo-dyed cotton (pl. 20). They also incorporate cotton dyed with *Purpura patula pansa* – a species of shellfish, or sea-snail. Currently exploited along the Pacific coast of southern Oaxaca, molluscs are picked off the rocks at low tide during the winter months. When dyers squeeze and blow on them, the snails give off a foamy secretion which is rubbed on to the cotton. Although the liquid is initially colourless, contact with the air makes it turn yellow, green and, ultimately, purple. After repeated washings shellfish-dyed yarn softens to a delicate lavender, but according to popular belief it never loses the tang of the sea. Garments featuring shellfish-dyed thread fetch high prices when sold to collectors; rumours even tell of women being attacked and robbed of their valuable striped skirts.

Today natural colourants are rarely used to tie-dye thread. Archaeological remains have confirmed the existence of *ikat* techniques in pre-Conquest Peru, but not thus far in Mexico. If not indigenous, procedures may have been introduced under Spanish rule, either from Southeast Asia or from the Middle East via Italy and Majorca. In recent years *ikat* methods for patterning sashes and

Pre-Hispanic spindle whorls of baked clay, decorated with stamped or incised designs. ABOVE *A jaguar.* OPPOSITE *A bird – the chachalaca, or roadrunner.*

quechquemitl have virtually disappeared from Otomí villages where they were once current, but yarn for *rebozos* is still tie-dyed as it was during the eighteenth and nineteenth centuries in a number of *mestizo* centres. Dyers stretch the yarn between two sticks, binding it tightly with thread at predetermined intervals. When the skein is dipped in dye, the covered portions are 'reserved'. Later this procedure can be repeated with dye of different colours. In Mexico the woven designs achieved with *ikat* are rarely figurative. Delicate reptilian markings, characteristically blurred where bindings have been penetrated by dye, are the most widely admired form of decoration. Santa María del Río, in the State of San Luis Potosí, has long been famous for its dappled shawls of imported silk, but less costly versions in cotton and rayon are similarly woven in this and other centres for use throughout Mexico.

Silk and wool substitutes, such as rayon and acrylic, have become increasingly popular since the 1960s. This world-wide trend was precipitated in Indian Mexico by shortages of traditional fibres, yet many weavers are glad to save labour by purchasing cotton as well as synthetic thread in a dazzling range of colours. Sadly, most low-cost factory fibres are neither long-lasting nor colour-fast. There may also be economic disadvantages. When weavers stop gathering and processing their own materials, they join the national economy and become vulnerable to inflation; spiralling prices in recent years have forced numerous women to economize on materials and so jeopardize the quality of work. Even purists admit, however, that new materials can have inspirational value. The Huichol, whose sashes and bags were formerly woven from undyed wool, have enthusiastically adopted acrylic yarns in luminescent shades of lime-green, acid yellow and shocking pink; these are frequently re-spun and matched in startling combinations. Commercial yarns, trimmings and aniline dyes are now sold in markets and village shops throughout Mexico. Together they have altered the appearance of many traditional garments and increased the range of decoration open to purchasers, who ingeniously combine modern materials with ancient skills such as weaving.

Woven textiles are made by interlacing one series of threads, known as the 'weft', with a second series of threads, known was the 'warp'. To save time and energy most advanced cultures have devised ways of dividing warp threads into two sets; during weaving these are raised alternately to creating an opening for the weft to pass through. In Mexico this purpose has been served for at least four thousand years by the backstrap loom. The apparatus is simple, with no rigid framework, but setting it up is a lengthy process. First the weaver must organize the warp, which is wound in a figure of eight on to a warping frame. This device often consists of upright stakes which are pushed into the ground or slotted into holes in a wooden frame. Before they are entered into the loom, warp threads are dipped in maize water to stiffen them.

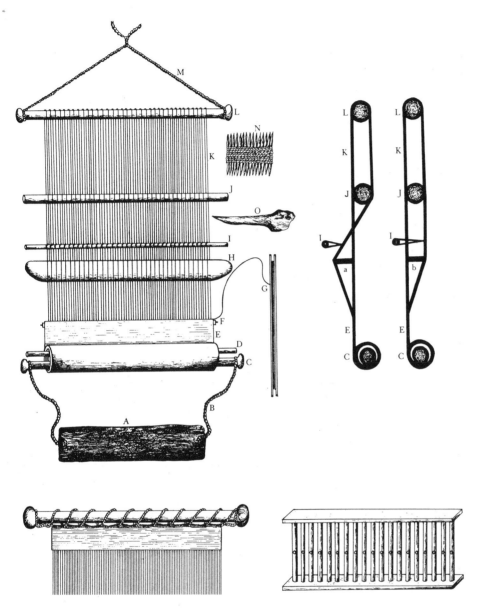

LEFT *The backstrap loom (telar de cintura). When not set up with warp threads, it is little more than a bundle of sticks of various sizes. Here (top left) the warp threads are wound directly round the loom bars to create cloth with side selvages only.*

A backstrap of leather B cord attaching the backstrap to the loom C front loom bar D rolling stick round which newly completed cloth is wound E web of woven cloth F tenter; often made from a hollow reed and held in place by thorns or nails, it is stretched across the underside of cloth to control the width G weft thread wound on to a shuttle stick H batten for enlarging the shed and the countershed, and for beating down the weft I stick heddle attached by loops of thread to selected warps J shed stick separating the two sets of alternate warp threads K warp threads L back loom bar M cord attaching loom to tree or post N comb for pushing down warp threads in narrow spaces O bone pick, occasionally used in pattern weaving to lift individual warp threads and to pull up or push down wefts.

(Top right) Warp threads shown in side view to demonstrate the weaving process. The shed stick (J) separates both sets of warp threads. The heddle (I) is attached to one set; when raised it pulls this set forward to form an opening called a 'shed' (a). After the passage of the weft, the first set drops behind the second set and forms the countershed (b). The weft, on its return journey through this second opening, passes over and under the same warps as the shed stick. (Bottom left) When warp threads are attached to the loom bars by cords, cloth with four selvages is produced. Weavers often begin a weaving with a short section, or 'heading', at one end; the loom is then reversed so that the weaving may be continued from the opposite end. This custom secures the spacing of the warps and prevents them from tangling. (Bottom right) Rigid heddle, used instead of a stick heddle in some sash-weaving villages. Stiff twigs, drilled in the centre with small holes and fixed to an upper and lower bar of wood, serve to support the warp threads.

Loom parts are made by the weaver and by members of her family. Dark interiors and lack of space lead most women to work outdoors. When the loom is in use, the bar furthest from the weaver is tied to a tree or post; the other is attached by a strap of leather or agave fibre to the weaver, who controls the tension of the tightly stretched warps with her body. The cross, created at the warping stage, forms the 'shed' and keeps each thread in its proper place (*see* diagram, above). Extremely long webs of cloth can be woven on the backstrap loom, but the width is limited by the weaver's armspan. When weaving lighter

Contemporary weaving constructions. The warp is drawn vertically and the weft horizontally.

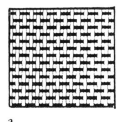 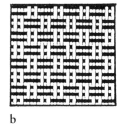

a   b

a Plain, or tabby. Each weft thread passes over and under one warp thread.

b Basket, or extended tabby. Warp and weft threads move in equal groups of two or more.

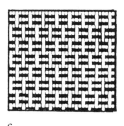 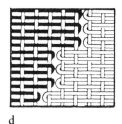

c   d

c Semi-basket. One element is more numerous than the other. Here two weft threads cross one warp thread.

d Tapestry. Cloth with one warp and a discontinuous weft composed of threads of different colours. These can meet in different ways. With kelim junctures (shown here) weft threads are turned back around warp threads to create vertical slits which are stepped to avoid weakening the cloth.

fabrics, women generally sit on a mat or low chair; heavy cloths can demand a kneeling or even a standing position.

The backstrap loom persists throughout most of Indian Mexico. It is also found in Central American countries such as Guatemala, which has a large Maya population. In the north of Mexico, however, there exists a second type of native loom. Square or rectangular in shape, the rigid loom is used today by the Tarahumara and the Northern Tepehuan of Chihuahua and by the Mayo of Sonora. Women from the first two groups are skilled weavers of heavy woollen blankets and sashes. They sit with their legs stretched out in front beneath the loom, which is built near ground level from four crudely finished logs. Woollen blankets are also the speciality of Mayo weavers. Four upright posts set in the ground support the end bars and necessitate a kneeling or squatting position.

Native looms may look 'primitive', but appearances are misleading. Their flexible and deceptively simple construction allows weavers to control threads manually and to achieve a range of effects which it would be hard to imitate on commercial looms. Clothing is often patterned during weaving, as it was in pre-Conquest times. Assembled without tailoring, Indian costume derives its elegance from the texture and decoration of the cloth itself, rather than from the simple though graceful lines of garments.

The interlacing of warp and weft results in a variety of cloth constructions. Plain weaving (a–c) allows the formation of warp and weft stripes, popular for skirts and *rebozos*. Textures can be modified: the introduction of thick or additional weft threads creates raised horizontal lines; alternatively, weavers can compress unnecessarily long rows of weft and produce puckered bands. Plain weaving has also given rise to more complex constructions, such as tapestry (d). With this technique warp threads are widely spaced and covered by weft threads of different colours, which do not travel the full width of the cloth, but move across selected areas only. Intricate geometric patterning is built up by this method on rigid and backstrap looms. Double weaving (e) requires great skill. Today it is done by the Otomí of Hidalgo, the Cora of Nayarit and their closely related neighbours, the Huichol. Bags and sashes are plain-woven, often with highly complex motifs, in two layers and two colours. Designs are identical on both sides of the cloth but the colours are reversed, so that a black eagle on a red background becomes a red eagle on a black background. Although the loom incorporates a minimum of parts during basic weaving, additional tools may be needed for pattern weaving.

The binding system for twill weaving is different from that used in plain weaving (f). By moving the points of intersection regularly to the right or left, backstrap weavers create diagonal lines in cloth. Twill techniques are often used to pattern woollen skirts and blankets with lozenges and zigzag motifs. Gauze weaving, for the creation of open-meshed cloth, has a wide distribution (g).

Construction methods differ from those examined so far, because selected warp threads are displaced: crossed by hand, they are secured by the weft. In the Puebla highlands Nahua backstrap weavers make *quechquemitl* with the delicacy of lace. Women in and around Cuetzalan rely on several heddles to divide warp threads into groups; in villages such as Atla or Xolotla, however, manipulations are largely manual, even during the creation of figured gauze featuring animals, double-headed birds and riders on horseback. Laborious finger manipulations are also required for the increasingly rare art of weft-wrap openwork (h). By winding one or more weft threads round several warp threads, backstrap weavers produce tiny openings in the cloth. Festive *huipiles* with bird, animal, flower and human motifs were exquisitely woven until recently in the Zapotec village of Santiago Choapan, Oaxaca.

The versatility of the backstrap loom is further demonstrated by curved weaving (i). Apparently unknown outside the Americas, this technique persists in a small number of Otomí, Nahua and Totonac villages in the Puebla highlands, where *quechquemitl* weavers convert selected warp threads to weft. Finished webs are shaped at one corner of one end; when two are joined, the result is a gently rounded garment. Warp patterning (j), achievable on both types of native loom, is a popular method for embellishing sashes. When warp threads are moved periodically over and under varying numbers of weft threads, raised geometric and figurative designs are created in the cloth.

Of the many decorative loom techniques still current in Mexico, however, the most popular is weft brocading (k). It is used for virtually all categories of Indian clothing and is often mistaken for embroidery by uninitiated observers. Combined with plain or gauze weaving, it relies on supplementary threads which are added to the ground weave. In most regions brightly coloured yarns are preferred, but weavers in a few communities specialize in brocading with white thread on a white background. Warp brocading is also practised in some villages for the elaboration of sashes. With weft-loop weaving (l), which is closely related to brocading, supplementary weft threads are pulled up with a pick to form a pattern of loops. Among the lowland Totonac of Veracruz and the highland Otomí of San Pablito, Puebla, this technique serves to create all-white *servilletas*, or cloths, of great beauty.

Indigenous weaving methods remain virtually exclusive to women. The Spanish treadle loom, by contrast, is worked by men. Despite the occasional addition of modern features, this loom is directly descended from medieval prototypes which appeared in Europe around AD 1000. By using foot pedals to form sheds automatically, weavers have the advantage of speed; they can also produce cloth webs that are wider and very much longer than those from native looms. Constructed by local carpenters, treadle looms are often found in small family-run workshops. Output includes skirt lengths, *rebozos* and blankets which are

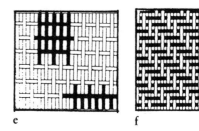

e *Double weaving. Two sets of differently coloured warp threads are used. Each warp thread is plain-woven with a weft thread of the same colour. The two layers of cloth are periodically interchanged.*

f *Twill. Diagonal lines are formed when warp threads are regularly positioned to the right or left of successive weft threads. Shown here is 2/2 twill, created if two warp threads pass over, then under, two weft threads.*

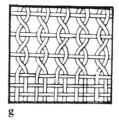
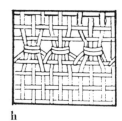

g *Gauze. Selected warp threads are crossed by hand and secured by the weft. This technique is usually combined with plain weaving, as here.*

h *Weft-wrap openwork. One or more weft threads are wrapped round a group of warp threads. Generally this technique is combined with plain weaving, as here.*

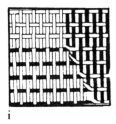
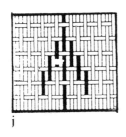

i   j

i Curved weaving. Some quechquemitl *weavers create shaped cloth by converting adjacent warp to weft threads.*

j Warp patterning. Warp threads cross varying numbers of weft threads to form patterns in the cloth.

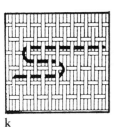
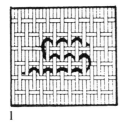

k   l

k Brocade patterning. Supplementary weft threads, which rarely travel across the whole web, create superstructural designs. Here weft brocading is combined with plain weaving.

l Weft-loop brocading. Supplementary weft threads are looped to form raised superstructural patterning.

bought by the local Indian population. Plain weaving may give stripes and checks; twill techniques, although less common, can pattern cloth with delicate lozenge designs. In addition many weavers of *sarapes* rely on tapestry methods to create fine woollen garments replete with geometric motifs, birds, horses and garlands of flowers. So skilful are the Zapotec of Teotitlán del Valle, Oaxaca, that they have for many years been reproducing the designs of Matisse, Escher and Miró as rugs and wall-hangings for foreign buyers. Isaac Vásquez García is not content to copy European models: his workshop now produces ambitious tapestry-woven scenes taken from pre-Hispanic murals and codices.

Embroidery, existent before the Conquest, received new impetus under Spanish rule. Today a wide range of stitches enables women to pattern home-woven cloth and to personalize bought fabrics with cotton, wool, acrylic, silk and rayon thread. In many regions garments display increasingly large areas of needlework, as brightly coloured factory yarns affect local tastes. Satin-stitched animals, birds, foliage and flowers adorn *huipiles*, skirts, blouses and *servilletas* in a number of villages; often this same stitch is used to join cloth webs decoratively. Running stitch, identifiable in pre-Conquest textile fragments, is equally popular, especially in the Puebla highlands, where Nahua women create exquisite blouses featuring roses, doves, horses and Virgins surrounded by decorative lettering. *Pepenado fruncido*, now rare, is a speciality amongst Otomí women in San Juan Ixtenco, Tlaxcala. Here tiny folds in the yoke and sleeves of blouses are secured by running stitches which form areas of negative patterning.

These embroidery techniques have been eclipsed in recent years, however, by cross and long-armed cross. Both stitches are used to great effect by the Huichol, who embellish male and female garments with double-headed eagles, deer and zigzag patterning. Looped stitches are found in communities such as Pinotepa Nacional in Oaxaca: here minutely chain-stitched crabs, fish and scorpions decorate the silk band which borders the neck of Mixtec wedding *huipiles*. In Cuetzalan, Puebla, the corners of gauze-woven Nahua *quechquemitl* are frequently embellished with feather stitching.

Couching, important in Colonial times when church textiles displayed a wealth of metallic thread, is still practised. With this technique, which is open to many variations, delicate threads are sewn to the ground material with other threads. This is the case in Acatlán, Guerrero, where Nahua women weave and embroider wrap-around skirts (pl. 16). The silken flowers and fanciful creatures that embellish these eye-catching garments can, in some cases, be seen only on Sundays and on festive occasions; during the rest of the year skirts are often worn inside-out for protection.

In many communities treadle-operated sewing machines serve to seam garments, but they can also provide decorative stitching. Skirts and blouses are enlivened in some villages by undulating borders and whirlpool designs; *huipiles* on the Isthmus of Oaxaca are often patterned with superimposed lines of chain stitch which have the delicacy of filigree, while skirts and *huipiles* in parts of Yucatán resemble colourful flower gardens satin-stitched in silk (pls 26, 32).

The art of embroidery is largely confined to women; like weaving, it is taught during late childhood. Designs are perpetuated by samplers, which serve as teaching aids but also act as reminders during adult life. Fine nineteenth-century samplers in London's Victoria and Albert Museum show not just embroidery but also drawn threadwork. Of European inspiration, this technique requires individual threads to be drawn out from the cloth; the remaining threads are then regrouped, bound to produce a square-meshed ground and reinforced with decorative stitching. Drawn threadwork is used today in many areas to embellish clothing, *servilletas* and tablecloths.

Lace-making, widely taught under Colonial rule, has been eclipsed by the spread of factory lace. During Zapotec festivals in Tehuantepec, however, elaborate head-dresses and richly embroidered skirts still feature wide flounces of genuine lace. Crochet is popular for trimming the neck and arm openings of blouses and *huipiles*; it is also used to create *servilletas*, blouse yokes and even *quechquemitl*. In Nahua villages such as Atla and Xolotla, Puebla, *quechquemitl* are patterned with plant and animal motifs to simulate traditional gauze-woven examples. Before the Conquest, garments sometimes had decorative fringing along their edges. This custom persists, enriched perhaps by similar Spanish styles. Weavers knot and braid uncut warp threads in a variety of ways (pl. 41). In some villages *rebozo* fringes even form figurative designs such as birds and animals. Alternatively fringes may be fashioned separately and sewn on to the edges of *quechquemitl* (pl. 34).

Rising prices are pushing beadwork beyond the reach of poorer families. This form of decoration, which achieved great popularity during the nineteenth century, makes garments extremely costly. In some regions, including the Puebla highlands, shimmering designs are created by sewing small glass beads on to the yokes and sleeves of blouses. This technique is also used to embellish men's gala shirts in the Otomí village of San Pablito. Beads may, in addition, be incorporated into areas of crochet on blouses or knotted into the fringes of *servilletas*.

There is no proof that finished cloth was tie-dyed before the Conquest. Until recently, however, the technique was applied in parts of Querétaro and Hidalgo. By binding sections of cloth before immersing it in dye, Otomí weavers would pattern skirts and small *sarapes* with flowers, dots and diamonds. Today only a few old women recall the procedure, but there is hope of a government-sponsored revival. *Batik*, which relies on wax to repel dye, was definitely employed in ancient times, albeit to an unknown degree. Today it is found nowhere in Indian Mexico, although city designers occasionally make use of the technique for tablecloths and Western-style clothing.

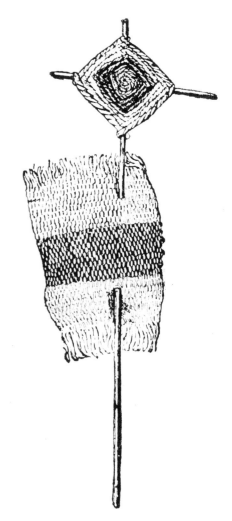

Huichol votive offering termed a tsikuri, *or* gods' eye. *The lozenge of coloured wool allows the gods to view their followers; the miniature weaving is a woman's request for divine aid during textile work.*

Clay stamps may once have served to pattern cloth (illus. p. 51); now wooden stamps print agave-fibre bags with simple designs in Huastec communities near Tantoyuca, Veracruz. Freehand painting, existent before the Conquest, is also favoured in various regions where agave-fibre shoulder-bags are decorated with brilliant aniline colours. Replete with lettering and fanciful creatures, such bags have great exuberance and charm (pl. 46).

Overpainting is an interesting custom which occurs in the Chinantec village of San Felipe Usila, Oaxaca (pl. 31). Here, densely and colourfully brocaded *huipiles* are partially coated with *fuchina* (an industrial purple colourant); when the investigator Carlota Mapelli Mozzi asked the reason for this, she was told that it 'to stop the sun from eating the colour of the threads'. Colour-transference is another rare and unusual method of decoration, whereby colours from patterned areas are deliberately imprinted on to plain areas. As has been said, commercial dyes often run when clothing is washed. Although the streaking of carefully woven or embroidered garments might be mourned by outsiders, however, the effects are accepted and even admired by Indian women.

Mexican appliqué achieved remarkable delicacy during the nineteenth century. With this ever-popular technique, additional cloth sections are stitched to the main cloth background. Brightly coloured shop-bought ribbons are laid flat on skirts, blouses, *huipiles* and *quechquemitl*, often concealing cloth joins. Hemmed into points, they also decorate neck openings. Ribbons have many uses apart from appliqué, however. They may be inserted between cloth webs, seamed together to provide frills or sleeves, fashioned into rosettes, or used to form rainbow cascades which hang from *huipiles* and hats.

Factory trimmings such as braid and lace also play a part in contemporary Indian costume, while sales of colourful factory cloth continue to rise. Aprons, blouses and skirts on waistbands, many featuring flounces, ruffles and tucks, are increasingly made from glistening rayons and sateens. *Huipiles* from Mazatec villages such as Huautla de Jiménez in Oaxaca are immensely eye-catching, yet demand little workmanship, since they are made almost entirely from lengths of cloth and machine lace which have been seamed together.

Love of ornamentation leads many Indian peoples to employ additional forms of decoration. In numerous communities tassels, pompons, sequins, non-functional buttons and even butterfly chrysalides are added to garments already replete with woven or embroidered motifs. It is this mixture of ancient and modern, of tradition and innovation, which lends such richness and vitality to Mexico's wide range of costumes.

In regions where festive styles differ from everyday styles, the range is increased still further. Throughout the highlands of Chiapas, for example, many women favour two kinds of *huipil*. On her wedding day a Tzotzil bride in Zinacantán lays aside her usual *huipil* in favour of a magnificent white *huipil* embellished by coloured weft threads interspun with white chicken down. Only here are feathers still incorporated into cloth as they were before the Conquest. Also in Chiapas, as in some other areas, the status of Indian dignitaries is symbolized during ceremonies by special items of dress; these include brocaded sashes which are worn about the neck by male officials from Tenejapa.

In many Indian societies it is impossible, even today, to separate the secular from the sacred. Among the Huichol, clothing has a spiritual as well as a functional role: designs, which serve as visual prayers, protect the wearer from harm and carry many layers of meaning; waist-sashes, which are identified with serpents because of their long, winding shape and because of the reptilian markings which they often display, serve as requests for rain and for the benefits which rain brings – namely good crops, health and long life. Colours and design motifs also retain their symbolic importance in the Chiapas highlands and in parts of Oaxaca, where the woven designs of sashes are believed by the coastal Mixtec to guard unborn children against 'The Rainbow of the East' and other evil forces.

In pre-Hispanic times idols were magnificently arrayed. Today, in the Tzotzil village of Magdalenas, in the Otomí village of San Pablito or in the Mazahua village of San Francisco Tepeolulco, the Virgin Mary is clothed with care and devotion in accordance with local costume styles. Some communities have even retained rituals linking infants with their future duties: in Zinacantán a male baby is given a digging stick and a hoe to hold, but a girl receives a *mano*, or pestle, for grinding food, and parts from a backstrap loom. Later, divine assistance may be sought: when adolescent daughters are learning to weave or embroider in parts of Chiapas, mothers offer candles in church and ask for help from the Virgin Mary and the female saints. In a non-Christian society like that of the Huichol, divine goodwill is also entreated: before embarking on textile work, women sometimes make votive offerings to the gods.

Women labour long hours to clothe themselves and their families. They take great pride in their skill, for they believe that they are contributing to the well-being of the community and playing their part in ensuring divine harmony. It is fitting, therefore, that the tools that accompany weavers throughout their lives should accompany them to the grave. In many Indian societies, death is still visualized as a long journey, for which the traveller must be prepared. In San Pedro Chenalhó, Chiapas, each woman is buried with a spindle, needle and thread so that she can mend her clothes on the voyage to the next world.

The textile arts, together with the beliefs and rituals that surround them, demonstrate a continuity with the past which is truly remarkable. It would be sad indeed if the long evolution of Mexican costume should end, over the next few decades, with the uniformity of Western dress. Change is inevitable, but civilization would be poorly served by the loss of textile skills that have endured for countless centuries since their origin in the New and Old Worlds.

17–20 *Details of women's garments woven on the backstrap loom.* TOP LEFT *Brocade-patterned Chinantec* huipil, *with an appliquéd section of ribbon, from San Lucas Ojitlán, Oaxaca. Area shown 27½" x 25½" (70 x 65 cm).* TOP RIGHT *Brocade-patterned* huipil *woven in Magdalenas, Chiapas, from naturally dyed wool. Colours and geometric designs convey elements of Tzotzil cosmology. Area shown 12" x 10⅝" (30.5 x 27 cm).* BOTTOM LEFT *Brocade-patterned* huipil *from the Tzotzil village of San Andrés Larrainzar, Chiapas. Area shown 9⅞" x 8⅞" (25 x 22.5 cm).* BOTTOM RIGHT *Mixtec skirt section with warp stripes from Pinotepa de Don Luis, Oaxaca. It incorporates cochineal-dyed silk, dark blue cotton dyed with indigo, and lilac cotton dyed with the secretion of shellfish. Area shown 27½" x 25½" (70 x 65 cm).*

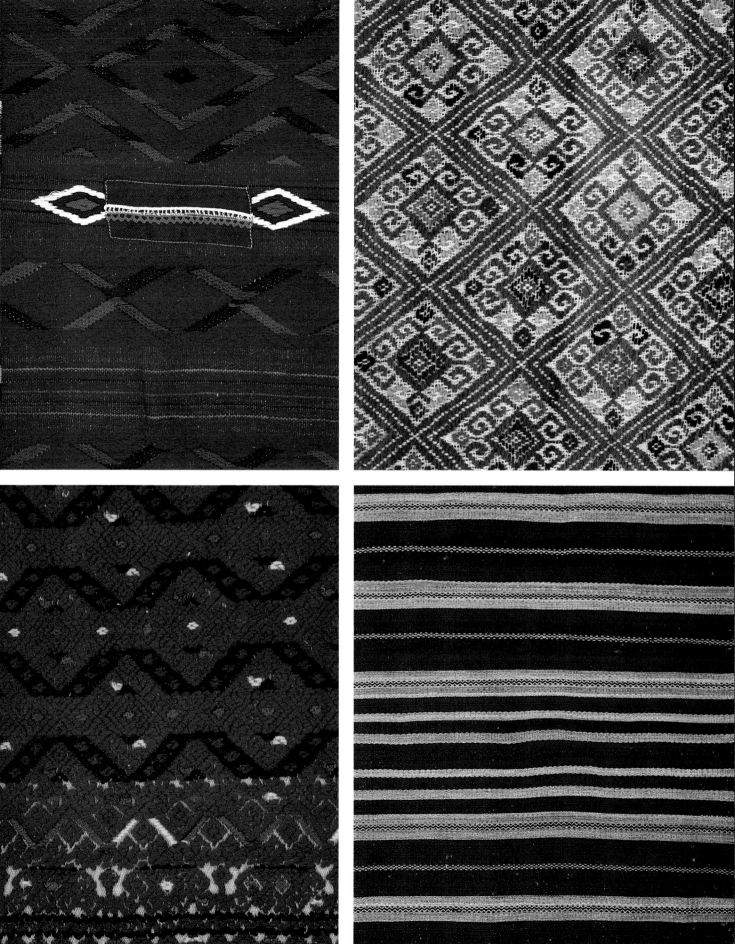

21 LEFT *Chatino blouse of factory-produced cotton cloth with cross-stitched motifs from Oaxaca. L 27" (68.6 cm).*

22–25 *Nahua blouses from the State of Puebla.* BELOW LEFT *The Virgin Mary, hand-embroidered in running stitch with acrylic yarn, from Coacuila. L 22" (56 cm).* BELOW RIGHT *Embroidered by Martina Cordoba Negrete*

from Chachahuantla, this blouse features satin-stitched flowers worked by hand and red swirling designs done by machine. L 23⅝" (60 cm). BOTTOM LEFT *Hand-embroidered in satin stitch with cotton thread. L 23¼" (59 cm).*

BOTTOM RIGHT *Embroidered by hand in running stitch with green wool and by machine with red cotton thread by María Antonia Martes of Huilacapixtla. L 20¼" (51.5 cm).*

26 LEFT *Neck area of a Maya* huipil *from Chichén Itzá, Yucatán. Factory-produced cotton cloth has been embroidered in satin stitch with synthetic silk thread on a sewing machine. Area shown 16½" sq. (42 cm sq.).*

27 BELOW *Dress of factory-produced cotton cloth. Sleeves, neck and yoke are trimmed in crochet. Floral designs were satin stitched in silk thread by Faustina Sumano de Sánchez of San Juan Chilateca, Oaxaca. W (including sleeves) 24" (61 cm).*

28, 29 European influence extended the range of Mexican motifs; many textiles now show imagery from the Catholic Church and non-indigenous animals such as horses. ABOVE Detail from a cotton servilleta (cloth) from San Miguel Ameyalco in the State of Mexico. Motifs are brocaded with acrylic threads on the backstrap loom by Otomí weaver Ana Cecilia Cruz Alberto. Area shown 25" sq. (63.5 cm sq.). RIGHT Bottom section of Huichol man's trouser leg from Jalisco. Factory cloth has been embroidered in cross stitch. Area shown 13⅜" sq. (34 cm sq.).

Serv*illeta section embroidered by Enriqueta Bernardino Gómez from the Mazahua village of San Felipe Santiago in the State of Mexico. Area shown 12¾" sq. (32.5 cm sq.).*

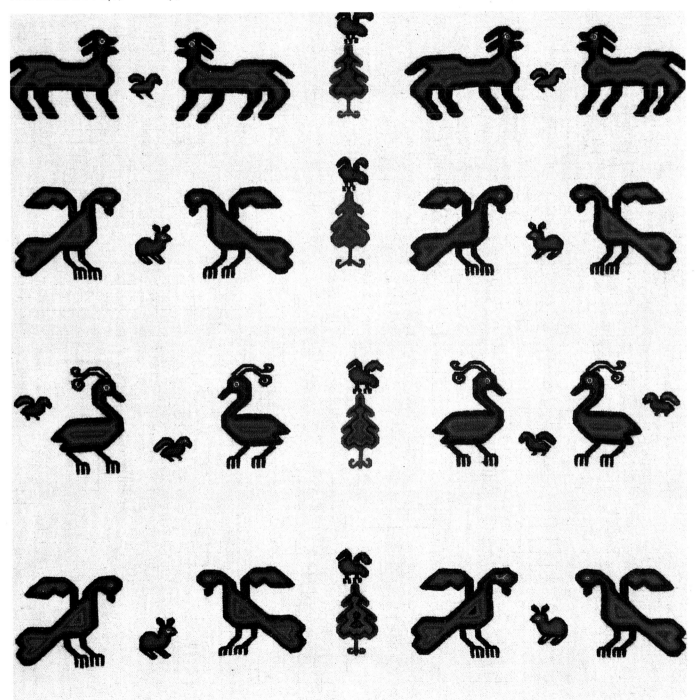

40

31 LEFT *Chinantec woven* huipil *from San Felipe Usila, Oaxaca, showing plain, gauze and brocade techniques. This three-web, knee-length woman's tunic has been partially over-painted. Lace and ribbons are factory made. Excluding sleeves 36⅝" x 27½" (93 x 70 cm).*

33 BELOW *Two-web Otomí* quechquemitl *with cross-stitched decoration from San Pablito, Puebla. Made from cotton and wool on a backstrap loom, it demonstrates the art of curved weaving. Each web 16¾" x 28⅛" (42.5 x 71.5 cm).*

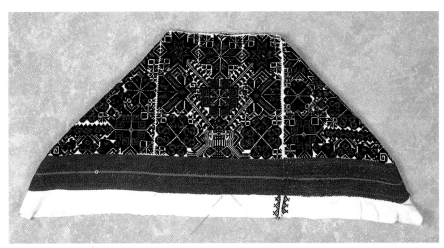

32 ABOVE *Zapotec* huipil *of black sateen from Tehuantepec, Oaxaca. Machine embroidered in chain stitch, this garment is short and close-fitting. 21¼" x 24¼" (54 x 61.5 cm).*

34 ABOVE *Fringed* quechquemitl *of acrylic yarn from the Mazahua village of San Francisco Tepeolulco in the State of Mexico. Woven in two webs on a backstrap loom, it was embroidered in cross stitch by Teresa Sánchez Galindo. Each web (excluding fringe) 11⅝" x 28" (29.5 x 71 cm).*

35, 36 Two satin-stitched servilletas of factory-produced cloth from the Otomí village of San Pablito, Puebla. LEFT The Virgin of Guadalupe. D approx. 26¾" (68 cm). BOTTOM LEFT A star design often found in textiles from this village. 27" x 34" (68.5 x 86.5 cm).

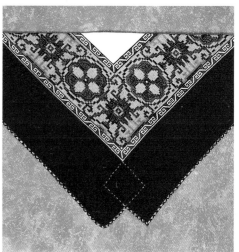

37, 38 Men's gala kerchiefs made from factory-produced cotton cloth. TOP Embroidered by Fredy Mendez in satin stitch, and embellished with glittering studs, from the Totonac community of El Tajín, Veracruz. W shown 15¾" (40 cm). ABOVE Embroidered in cross stitch and edged with flannel from a Huichol community in Jalisco. W shown 23⅝" (60 cm).

39 Servilleta *of factory cotton cloth*
embroidered in satin stitch with Otomí spirits
from San Pablito, Puebla. 30⅛" x 34"
(76.5 x 86.5 cm).

40 BELOW *Waist-sashes of wool, acrylic and cotton, with warp patterning and warp brocading. The male sash shown fourth from the top was woven on a Tarahumara log loom in the State of Chihuahua. All other sashes were created for female use by Otomí and Mazahua weavers on backstrap looms in the states of Mexico and Querétaro. H of area shown 30″ (76.1 cm).*

41 BELOW *Ikat-patterned* rebozo *(shawl) of artificial silk with finger-knotted fringes from Santa María del Río, San Luis Potosi. H of area shown 26″ (66 cm).*

42 RIGHT *Warp-patterned shoulder-bag woven on a backstrap loom from commercial cotton thread by Crispina Navarro Gómez in the Zapotec village of Santo Tomás Jalieza, Oaxaca. 9⅝″ x 9″ (24.5 x 23 cm).*

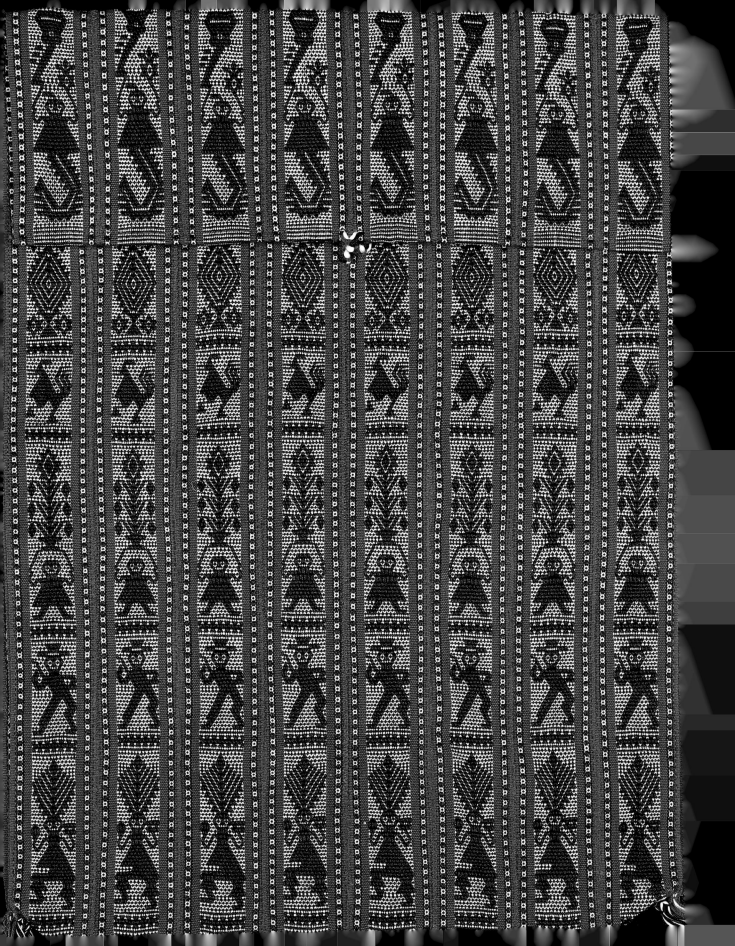

43, 44 *Huichol shoulder-bags of netted beadwork from Jalisco.* LEFT *Double-headed eagles, bead droplets and a cloth backing.* 6⅜" x 5¾" (16.2 x 14.6 cm). BELOW *Pompons of acrylic yarn.* 17" sq. (43.2 cm sq.).

45 TOP RIGHT *Huichol shoulder-bags, double-woven on a backstrap loom with hand-spun, undyed wools in Jalisco. Smallest bag* 8½" x 11" (21.5 x 28 cm); *largest* 13⅛" x 15⅜" (33.5 x 39 cm).

46 RIGHT *Shoulder-bags woven on the backstrap loom from agave fibre, and purchased in the states of Puebla and Guerrero. Painted decoration has been done freehand with aniline colourants. Bag inscribed* Amor Infiel *(Faithless Love)* 13½" x 12" (34.3 x 30.5 cm).

CHAPTER III

JEWELRY AND ADORNMENT

BEFORE THE CONQUEST copper, gold and silversmiths were highly regarded. They knew how to weld and to 'marry' gold with silver, to inlay or encrust, to plate copper with gold, and to obtain elaborate repoussé designs by chiselling metals to paper thinness. They also cast by the 'lost wax' method: tiny bells and other ornaments were modelled from clay and finely ground charcoal, coated with wax, then enclosed in clay. When moulds were baked, the wax was melted out through a hole in the base, leaving a cavity for molten metal; afterwards casts were broken and finished objects removed for polishing. Although metal-working seems to have originated in Ecuador or Peru, Mixtec grave goods from Monte Albán reveal the artistry of native jewelers: entombed in the fourteenth century were finger-rings with eagles, exquisite necklaces, turquoise mosaics and lost-wax pendants depicting gods and sacred symbols. Sadly, the Conquest heralded the destruction of most such treasures.

In 1519, when Aztec civilization was at its height, the emperor Moctezuma was alarmed by reports from the Gulf Coast of seaborne mountains. These were Spanish ships carrying Hernán Cortés and his followers from the Old World to the New. Believing them to be gods, Moctezuma summoned metalsmiths and lapidaries. Rich gifts sent to greet the fair-skinned travellers included gold orna-ments in the form of ducks and monkeys, a sun-shaped gold disk as big as a cartwheel, and a larger moon-shaped disk of silver. For Fray Bartolomé de las Casas, who saw them in Seville, these things were 'so rich, and made and worked with such artifice, that they seemed a dream and not fashioned by the hands of men'. Most *conquistadores* were not interested in artistry, however. With sur-prise the Aztec noted the reactions of their visitors: 'When they were given presents the Spaniards burst into smiles; their eyes shone with pleasure. . . . They picked up the gold and fingered it like monkeys; they seemed to be trans-ported by joy, as if their hearts were illuminated and made new. . . .'

During the years that followed the Conquest, countless examples of native goldwork were melted down. Mining methods, which had been rudimentary, were re-organized: Indians were sent to work underground in inhuman condi-tions. European processes were introduced, and guilds for jewelers instituted; for a time Indian craftsmen were barred from working, using or possessing the precious metals of their land; only later were they instructed in Spanish working methods.

Mexico's wealth, which rested chiefly on shipments of gold and silver, was reflected in the baroque opulence of its churches. Roofs and *retablos* were of

47 LEFT *Necklaces incorporating seeds and beads of stone, clay and glass. The top rows show* papelillo*: these paper-thin glass beads are worn in many Indian villages. Area shown approx. 9⅞" sq. (25 cm sq.).*

solid gold. Priceless gifts were bestowed on images of the Virgin Mary: Nuestra Señora de los Remedios, the patroness of Spaniards in Mexico, even had a special treasurer to look after her collection of jewels. Eighteenth-century portraits offer few representations of Indians, but show wealthy female sitters dressed in European fashion with loops and bowknots of gold and diamonds, pearl necklaces, bracelets and earrings; men wore diamond coat buttons and shoe buckles, and cravats set with precious stones and pearls.

After Independence an influx of European travellers left descriptions of high-society wealth. Frances Calderón de la Barca complained of 'a monotony of diamond earrings'. Sir Edward B. Tylor was struck by the flashy apparel of the Mexican *charro*, or horseman: 'it is now hardly respectable', he noted wryly, 'to have more than a few pounds worth of bullion on one's saddle or around one's hat, or to wear a hundred or so of buttons of solid gold down the sides of one's trousers'.

In the wake of the Revolution came a new respect for Mexico's Indian heritage and for the national culture. In her daily life the painter Frida Kahlo wore *rebozos* and *huipiles*, and decked herself out with pre-Hispanic bead necklaces and earrings of heavy silver or gold filigree. Her fondness for Mexican jewelry even made its mark in Europe: Frida Kahlo's hand, with her customary profusion of rings, was used on the cover of *Vogue*. The prevailing enthusiasm for ancient cultures and Mexican motifs was shared by a number of jewelry designers; from the 1920s they began increasingly to supply a tourist market, and the styles which they forged are still thought of today in many parts of the world as characteristically 'Mexican'.

The pioneering work of Frederick Davis and William Spratling from North America, and the achievements of their successors, are discussed by Mary L. Davis and Greta Pack in their book *Mexican Jewelry*. At a time when Mexican women were mostly wearing gold, Spratling and his peers concentrated on silver; with the exception of polished obsidian and amethyst quartz, stones were rarely used. The distinctive quality of hand-made articles was prized. Today Taxco in Guerrero is often described as the centre of Mexican jewelry production, yet before Spratling's arrival in 1929 this important mining town had few jewelers. His successful training programme started a trend; today there are hundreds of silversmiths in Taxco. Their jewelry echoes many of the pre-Hispanic designs published in 1947 by Jorge Enciso in his influential book *Sellos Antiguos de México*. At their hackneyed worst, however, ornaments rely repetitively on the Aztec calendar stone and on the stepped fret which has so often been re-worked by Western designers in recent years.

Mexican jewelry production is not limited to Taxco, and it is hard to chart the development of the many localized styles, which may draw on Indian, Spanish, Moorish or Chinese traditions. The rise of filigree work in Colonial times is

ABOVE *Pre-Conquest Mixtec lip-plug of gold, from Oaxaca.* OPPOSITE *Motifs made by pre-Conquest pottery stamps, excavated in Mexico City. They show a fire serpent (top) and a monkey. Stamps may have been used in ancient Mexico to pattern cloth. Highly stylized motifs of this type, published in 1947 by Jorge Enciso, have inspired many jewelry designers.*

sometimes attributed to Chinese influence, yet techniques mirror those employed in Spain. For openwork filigree, jewelers require a minimum of metal: delicately twisted wires may make up less than half the surface; the rest is air.

The city of Oaxaca is one of several places where filigree is worked in gold. Before prices began to rise in the 1970s, 14 or 18 carat gold was popular, but 12 carat is more usual today. Melted in a crucible and forged on an anvil, the alloyed gold is reduced to wire of two sizes. When soldered, heavy (frame) and light (filler) wires form a lace-like pattern. Traditional designs include *el jardín* (the garden), *el ramo* (the branch) and *el gusano* (the worm). Jewelry made by Fausto Vargas Ramírez incorporates pearls and coral in traditional fashion. Frequently earrings are plated with 24 carat gold; the bright yellow tones which result are admired locally, but not always understood by foreign tourists, who are accustomed to lower alloys of a darker hue. In the Oaxaca Valley Zapotec women often regard their earrings as an investment against hard times; thinking them to be inexpensive trinkets tourists sometimes ask the price, only to react with amazement when the true value is revealed.

Representations of native gods were proscribed after the Conquest, and replaced by symbols of the Catholic faith. In Yucatán long rosaries and crosses of gold filigree are proudly worn during festivals by *mestizo* women. The introduction of coins also had a strong impact; on the Isthmus near Tehuantepec, many Zapotec women display their savings during festivals in the form of chokers, bracelets, rings, earrings and heavy coin necklaces of gold or dipped silver.

During their march to the Aztec capital, the Spaniards encountered Totonac men with gold lip-rings and other ornaments. Today gold jewelry is much prized by Totonac women near Papantla, Veracruz. Marriage requires a bridegroom to bestow numerous gifts on his bride; these include a ring, earrings and a necklace of gold. When civil and church rites have been held in Papantla, a wedding feast is celebrated within the community. During the opening ceremony, the bride's everyday dress is removed in front of her parents' altar; she is then clothed in a white, Western-style dress and veil, and decked out in her new jewelry.

Successive Totonac generations have bought their jewelry in Papantla at La Bola de Oro (The Golden Ball). Founded in 1879 by Genaro Vargas Tapia, this enticing shop still stocks a sparkling array of 14 carat gold ornaments made on the premises. Some purchasers prefer to commission work, selecting the different elements according to personal taste. Earrings feature tiny hands, hearts, doves and baskets of flowers, soldered together in different combinations.

Exquisite earrings of silver, comprising different sections, are similarly worked in Tlatlauqui, Puebla (pls 52, 53). With consummate artistry Julio Angel Valera also assembles elaborately jointed fish, riveted scale by scale so that they move in the style of pre-Conquest figures. Casting is done with sand which has been moistened, then left to dry to the correct consistency. Contained by an outer framework in two facing blocks, the sand retains the shape of lead models. Liquid silver is poured through a narrow channel into the cavity; solidified sections are polished and chased. Soldering is done with a kerosine lamp: by blowing down a narrow mouth blowpipe, the jeweler directs the flame. As with other crafts, jewelry of extraordinary refinement is achieved with rudimentary tools and methods.

Worn by young and old alike, earrings are the most popular form of female adornment, and the ears of babies are pierced at birth. Local variations abound, many hung with small droplets which move and catch the light (pls 49, 53). Additional decoration may be provided by coloured stones. The skill of jewelers in Guanajuato is widely acknowledged. Earrings feature miniature leaves, flowers and birds of tooled gold or silver; supported on wires, they are accompanied by a profusion of turquoise beads. Birds' wings are encrusted with even smaller beads, and their eyes represented by minuscule ruby-red stones. Crescent-shaped earrings, known as *arracadas*, occur in many regions (pls 50, 51). Of Moorish and Spanish inspiration, many are wholly or partially filigree.

Sometimes silver ornaments are used to create necklaces. Gleaming fish, cast in silver, are combined with red glass beads in Pátzcuaro, Michoacán (pl. 57). Silver ornaments and charms, once worn in several Mixtec communities and in the Zapotec village of Santiago Choapan, are still made by the Armengol family on the outskirts of Oaxaca city. Here turkeys, alligators, rabbits and prancing horses are cut from sheet metal, shaped and engraved (pl. 54). Ornate compound crosses, up to seven inches in height, are also produced by silversmiths in Oaxaca city. Usually known as 'Yalalag crosses', after the Zapotec village of San Juan Yalalag, they feature a central cross with three pendant crosses. Much admired by tourists, such crosses have been largely abandoned by Indian women, who prefer more 'modern' forms of adornment.

Bracelets are rare in Indian Mexico. Silver rings with hearts and clasped hands, which pledge friendship or seal an engagement, are occasionally worn by *mestizo* women. In general, however, bracelets and rings are made for city-dwellers and tourists. Male decoration centres on the *charro*, descended from the horsemen of earlier times. Clothing worn during equestrian displays includes elaborate belt-buckles and cast or repoussé ornaments of silver. Amozoc in Puebla has long been a manufacturing centre for the trappings of *charrería*. Buttons, buckles, spurs, stirrups, knife-handles and pistol casings are traditionally rendered in silver and iridescent blued steel. The national figure of the *mariachi* is more recent in origin. With their wide-brimmed hats and tight-fitting suits decked out in silver buttons, *mariachi* musicians offer a romanticized vision of Mexico beloved of tour-operators but also of many Mexicans.

Sometimes jewelers are asked to make ex-votos, commonly called *milagros*, or miracles (pl. 56). Intended as an expression of thanks after divine interven-

*Earrings made in Pátzcuaro, Michoacán.
Different styles distinguish women from
different villages around the lake.*

tion, these often take the form of arms, legs, eyes and other parts of the body
cured through prayer. Alternatively they may represent domestic animals,
hearts, houses, cars and maize cobs. One nineteenth-century ex-voto, from a
private collection, is shaped like a jail with a padlock on the door. Although
milagros were formerly of gold or silver, cheaper metals are now more usual.
Price rises have similarly forced many metalsmiths to use tin or nickel for the
making of jewelry.

Before the Conquest the lapidary arts flourished. Turquoise, obsidian, rock
crystal and onyx were worked in Mexico, but the stone most generally esteemed
was *chalchihuitl*, or jade. Its uses were manifold: bead necklaces, pendants,
ornaments for nose and ears, ceremonial masks, axes and figurines were exquisitely and laboriously carved with the aid of string and an abrasive powder
such as sand, and with tubular drills made from hollow reeds or bird bones.
Prized for its medicinal qualities and its green hue, reminiscent of life-giving
water and vegetation, jade was valued above gold.

Today the exact source of nephrite (often referred to as 'true jade') is not
known. Green stones which are commonly sold as 'Mexican jade' are usually
jadeite, serpentine or dyed calcite. Serpentine, in a variety of shades, and other
minerals are skilfully worked by lapidaries in towns such as Iguala, Guerrero:
using electrically powered tools, they fashion handsome pendants and zoomorphic rings. Skulls, which echo pre-Hispanic examples, may be worked in amethyst or rock crystal (pl. 11). In the city of Querétaro, opals from nearby mountains are polished, together with other semi-precious stones such as agate and
'tiger's eye'. The extracting and cutting of these stones for national consumption
and export represent an important source of income for innumerable Mexicans.

Organic substances such as coral and pearls, although found off the coast of
Mexico, are frequently imported, and jewelry prices are correspondingly high.
The protective powers of coral are summed up by a popular saying: *coral contra
envidia y el mal* ('coral against envy and evil'). According to some Zapotec, it
can absorb the wearer's illness, paling visibly in the process.

Among the gifts offered to Cortés were elaborate necklaces of shells. Today
fragments of shell are sometimes engraved to emulate Maya adornments. Abalone shell, admired for its iridescent brilliance, is combined with metal by jewelers in Taxco, and inlaid in juniper wood by the Otomí of El Nith, Hidalgo (pls
48, 100). Tortoiseshell, from the hawksbill turtle, is occasionally worked on the
Yucatán Peninsula and bought by tourists (pl. 48). Hair ornaments, combs and
earrings of cow horn, carved into a profusion of forms, are the speciality of
villagers in San Antonio de la Isla, State of Mexico (pls 48, 80, 103).

Jet is fossilized vegetable matter: popular for the making of rosary beads, it is
also incorporated into necklaces and earrings in parts of Guerrero. Jet fragments, sold in Iguala market, are thought to confer good fortune on the wearer.

Considerable powers are also attributed to amber – the fossilized resin of coniferous trees which grew many thousands of years ago. Found inland in the State of Chiapas, amber is generally thought of as yellow, but it can also veer towards white, green and black. Some pieces feature air bubbles and small insects. For many generations amber amulets have been carved in Simojovel; shaped into hearts, hands, droplets and flower buds, they are often tied about the necks and wrists of small children to protect them from harm. In recent years, however, new veins have been discovered. San Cristóbal de las Casas has become a centre for itinerant jewelry-makers: female tourists from Europe and the USA are targeted as prospective purchasers by exotically garbed *mestizo* youths selling earrings, pendants and fine necklaces of polished and unpolished amber.

In some marginal communities distinctive styles of adornment persist, linking inhabitants with a pre-industrial age. Tarahumara and Seri women continue to make necklaces and earrings from seeds, shells, pieces of reed and tiny balls of wood or clay, while polished fish vertebrae, wooden carvings, small bones and toucan beaks are among the embellishments traditionally favoured by Huave and Lacandón women (pl. 61). In less remote areas interesting folk-jewelry is sometimes sold at fairs. Tiny lacquered gourds and painted wooden dishes are made up into earrings in Guerrero and Michoacán.

Glass was introduced into Mexico at the time of the Conquest. Bernal Díaz del Castillo's account of the Spanish landing is punctuated by references to gifts of glass beads; in return for gold and silver, these were offered to emissaries and local chiefs, who were reportedly delighted with the exchange! Early beads, used in trade, reached some of the remotest corners of Oaxaca. In San Pedro Quiatoni necklaces of Venetian glass have been passed down from generation to generation, while a few Mixe women in Mixistlán and Yacochi still wear twenty or more strands of beads which together weigh up to 3lb (1.6 kg). These majestic necklaces include numerous white beads of opaque glass which may have come from China on the Manila galleons. Sadly younger women are losing interest in these heirlooms; many have been sold to private collectors and museums.

Although modern glass beads never match the splendour of earlier examples, they are avidly bought by Indian women throughout Mexico (pl. 47). Lacandón women and small girls in Najá take pride in displaying as many necklaces as possible; sometimes these are hung with shiny safety-pins, foreign coins and door-keys. In Guerrero glass beads have become the sole distinguishing feature for the identically dressed Nahua of Zitlala and Acatlán: whereas inhabitants of the first village favour a single string of red beads, those from the second prefer a single string of imitation yellow amber. *Papelillo*, introduced into Mexico at the close of the last century, exerts a strong appeal; despite rising prices, many Indian women continue to deck themselves with these brilliantly painted beads of paper-thin glass, and to secure the various strands with colourful ribbons.

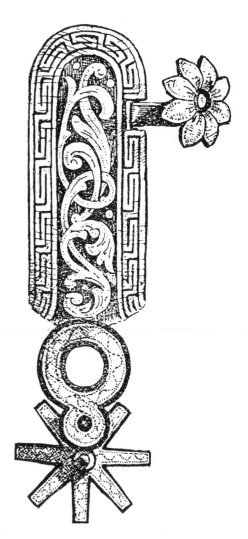

Spurs from the State of Puebla. These and other trappings for horsemen are made in the town of Amozoc, where they are cast and forged from steel. Metal is blued by heat treatment and inlaid with silver. The deep blue colour is described by the term pavón *(literally, 'peacock').*

Huichol man in San Andrés Cohamiata, Jalisco, wearing a pectoral and bracelet of netted beadwork; his shoulder-bag and shirt are richly embroidered. He is painting his face before a festival.

The Huichol have an especial fondness for glass beads. Cut off from the outside world by mountain peaks and deep canyons, they inhabit one of the remotest and most rugged parts of Mexico. This region, which covers just over a thousand square miles, stretches into the states of Jalisco, Nayarit, Durango and Zacatecas. Among the Huichol, distinctions are never made between the sacred and the profane; life, from the cradle to the grave, is invested with a symbolism which is often hard for outsiders to interpret. Religious belief, discussed in Chapter VII, is often expressed through clothing and ornament. Small glass beads are netted to form hat-bands, shoulder-bags, belts, necklaces with pendants, arm-bands, earrings and rings (pls 43–44, 58–60). Worn by men and women, these carry a profusion of designs which are drawn from nature. Popular jewelry motifs include antlered deer, scorpions, butterflies, squirrels, vines and squash plants. Zigzag lines that suggest lightning are associated with rain, together with double water-gourds, while the white *totó* flower that grows during the wet, maize-producing season is both a petition for and a symbol of maize. Another popular motif is the eagle. Thought to guard the young maize, it may be shown in profile with a single head or from the front with two heads to represent both profiles.

The art of netted beadwork is also practised by the Otomí of San Pablito, Puebla. On ceremonial occasions men's hats may be decorated with bands featuring zoomorphic designs, while women use colourful hair-cords of wool and beads. Sometimes tiny beaded sachets of aromatic herbs are hung about the neck to combat *los malos aires*, or bad airs, which are thought to carry disease. The sacred role still played by some Indian jewelry is underlined in communities where adornment, like clothing, is used during ceremonies to indicate status. In parts of the lowland Mixteca and the Chiapas highlands, special necklaces are worn by male and female dignitaries (illus. p. 20).

When Carl Lumholtz, the Norwegian anthropologist, visited Mexico towards the end of the last century, he noted the spread of 'cheap tawdry jewellery'. The intervening decades have intensified this trend; in any modern market the busiest stall is often one that carries a supply of plastic and gilt trinkets. The shift away from traditional jewelry is partially due to rising prices; alternatively it may be motivated by a desire for 'modernity' and, quite simply, by a love of exuberance and colour. Plastic hair-combs, slides and necklaces have been adopted in quantity by many Totonac and Tzeltal girls. Other ornaments, bought from healers and herbalists, or from vendors outside churches, incorporate fragments of real or fake coral and amber, seeds known as *ojo de venado* (deer's eye), images of the Virgin Mary or the Buddha, and cabbalistic symbols. These serve as amulets and talismans.

In the meantime the tourist market continues to inspire a range of non-traditional jewelry. Earrings and adornments of plaited raffia are an innovation in Santa María Chigmecatitlán, Puebla (pl. 55), while a recent order from the USA has given rise in Amozoc to imaginative pottery necklaces (pl. 10). In cities itinerant jewelry-makers are also responsible for an array of adornments: incorporating feathers, copper and other elements, these are often spread out on pavements to attract passers-by. 'Ethnic' fashions, discarded during the early 1970s, seem currently to be undergoing a revival in Europe and the USA. Heavy silver pendants and exotic earrings are once again featured in magazines by models promoting the 'Frida Kahlo look'. For a few years at least the jewelers of Mexico are likely to benefit from this trend.

Chapetas. *Such ornaments are still worn in pairs by* charros, *or horsemen, on their large felt hats.*

48 Earrings are the most popular form of female adornment and incorporate a wide range of materials. (All measurements include the earpiece). Top row: (left) glass beads and copper wire; Papantla, Veracruz. L 3½" (9 cm); (centre) glass beads with imitation gold coins and pearls; the colours used are those of the Mexican flag. L 3" (7.5 cm); (right) peacocks of tortoiseshell; Campeche. L 3¾" (9.5 cm).

Middle row: (left) cannabis leaves of painted horn; San Antonio de la Isla, State of Mexico. L 2" (5.1 cm); (centre) swordfish of painted horn; San Antonio de la Isla, State of Mexico. L 2½" (6.5 cm); (right) netted glass beadwork; San Pablito, Puebla. L 2⅜" (6 cm). Bottom row: (left) painted tin; Oaxaca city. L 2⅜" (6 cm); (right) wood inlaid with abalone shell; El Nith, Hidalgo. L 2⅜" (6 cm).

49 *Silver earrings from the states of Michoacán, Puebla and Mexico. Movement is a key feature. Earrings of this type are often inset with glass beads. Average H (including earpiece) 2⅛″ (5.5 cm).*

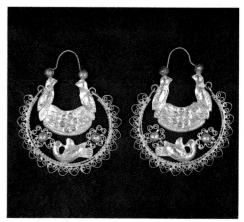

50, 51 *Silver repoussé earrings from the State of Mexico.* TOP *H (including earpiece) 2⅞″ (7.3 cm).* CENTRE *H (including earpiece) 2⅜″ (6 cm).*

52 ABOVE *Silver earrings by Julio Angel Valera from Tlatlauqui, Puebla. Those on the left display the national emblem of Mexico, supported by a tiny hand. H (including earpiece) 2¾″ (7 cm). The fish are jointed. H (including earpiece) 3⅛″ (8 cm).*

53 Silver earrings from various states. Sections have been cast in sand; birds, leaves, flowers and hands are all popular elements. Dangling droplets provide further decoration. The earrings shown top left were made by Julio Angel Valera from Tlatlauqui, Puebla. H (including earpiece) 2½" (6.2 cm).

54 *Necklace of red glass beads and repoussé silver ornaments from Oaxaca city. Horse 1⅛″ x 2¼″ (3 x 5.7 cm).*

56 BELOW *Milagros, or votive offerings, of gold. Made by jewelers, these give a visual form to people's prayers, and are pinned to the robes of saints in churches. H approx. 1⅛" (3 cm).*

57 BOTTOM *Necklace of silver fish and glass beads; Pátzcuaro, Michoacán. L of fish 1⅜" (3.5 cm).*

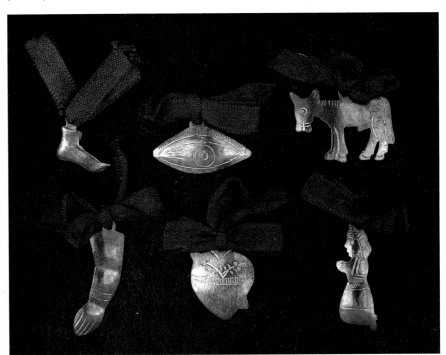

55 *Earrings of interwoven raffia from Santa María Chigmecatitlán, Puebla. H (including earpiece) 2¾" (7 cm).*

58 Netted Huichol jewelry of glass beads, for men as well as women, from San Andrés Cohamiata and other communities in the State of Jalisco. Included are belts, hat-bands, armbands, pectorals and earrings. Average L of earrings 2¾″ (7 cm).

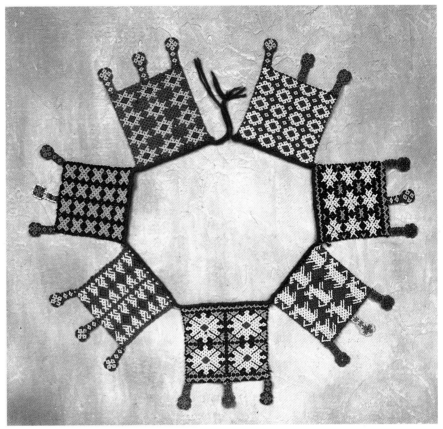

59 LEFT *Huichol man's netted pectoral of glass beads from Jalisco. H (from top of square to bottom of droplets) 5½" (14 cm).*

60 BELOW *Huichol man's ceremonial netted belt of glass beads from Jalisco. L of belt 28" (71 cm).*

61 RIGHT *Necklaces of carved wood, seeds and fish vertebrae from the Huave community of San Mateo del Mar, Oaxaca. Wooden ornaments are inspired by nature. H of bat (bottom left) 3" (7.5 cm).*

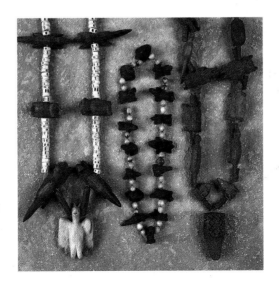

CHAPTER IV

CERAMICS

THE ART OF POTTERY goes back many thousands of years in the New World, and demonstrates an astonishing range of imaginative skills. Probably no other continent has achieved such diversity of form and decoration. In the West clay has often been considered a substance inferior to stone or wood for plastic expression. In the Americas, however, it has afforded works of supreme artistry. Pottery-making, in the opinion of archaeologists such as G.C. Vaillant, was the greatest of all pre-Columbian crafts.

By 1200 BC the rise of settled farming communities in the Valley of Mexico had fostered an abundance of pottery figurines and utensils. Creations in clay from Tlatilco, dated to between 1200 BC and 900 BC, are among the most aesthetically satisfying ever produced in Mexico. Over subsequent centuries clay was transformed by different peoples into water storage jars, pots of varying shapes and sizes, dishes, spindle whorls, jewelry, musical instruments such as flutes and rattles, incense burners, ritual vessels, funerary urns, idols, roof ornaments for temples, and figurines depicting animals, birds and human beings often engaged in everyday activities. On sale in the great Aztec marketplace, seen by Bernal Díaz del Castillo in 1519, was a vast array of 'pottery of all kinds, from big water-jars to little jugs, displayed in its own place'. The following lines, translated from Náhuatl, reveal the high esteem in which potters were held:

He who animates the clay
with penetrating eye amasses
and shapes it.
The good potter
puts effort into things,
teaches the clay to lie,
converses with his very heart,
breathes life into objects, creates,
knowing everything as if he were a Toltec,
he makes his hands dextrous.
The bad potter
dull-witted, clumsy in his art,
seems dead in life.

62 LEFT *Mermaid with aquatic creatures, decorated with commercial paints and varnished, from the workshop of Heriberto Castillo in Izúcar de Matamoros, Puebla. H 8⅝" (22 cm).*

In the absence of written records, modern investigators use ceramics to situate Mexico's ancient civilizations in time and space, and to define the relationships that existed between them. Because pottery is both abundant and immune to decay, it has become the backbone of archaeological research. Not only does it inform us about the way people lived and worshipped, but its frequent inclusion in burials also tells us about their expectations for an afterlife.

Today Mexico is still a land of potters. The ingenuity and skill of their Indian forebears have not been lost. Once a week, in rural areas, potters set out before dawn for market. Protected by deep baskets or swathed in dry grasses and corn husks, fragile wares are transported by mule and bus, or carried on the backs of their creators. In remote communities, where the pattern of life has changed very little, pottery is still needed for cooking, eating and storage. Often water has to be fetched from a spring or public tap. Many Indian homes have water jars and cooking pots whose basic shape has barely altered in centuries. Other ancient utensils include the *comal*, which is a flat, round griddle for heating *tortillas*; a bowl termed a *molcajete*, which has a roughened bottom for grating chilli peppers and similar foods; and *pichanchas*, or colanders, for straining maize. Although cooking is usually done indoors, the arms of a nearby cactus or the branches of a bush may serve as a natural outdoor support for pots. Ceremonial objects such as incense burners have also retained their traditional importance.

Illustration from the Codex Florentino *showing a farmer storing grain in pottery jars. Similar jars are used for storage today.*

Techniques and styles of decoration have proved as enduring in some communities as the forms and functions just described. In the purest Indian tradition are earthenware vessels and figurines which are hand modelled and fired under rudimentary conditions. The Lacandón who live at Najá, in the Chiapas rainforest, are the least acculturated of Mexico's many Maya peoples. Unlike most other Indian groups, they have never adopted Christianity. Lacandón women may occasionally fashion human figures, birds and animals which are fired in the ashes of the open fire, but men are usually responsible for the creation of ceremonial objects. These include clay drums with the head of Kayum, the god of song. Incense burners, each adorned with the face of a different deity, are painted with soot, lime and annatto juice. Throughout the year offerings are made to the censers, which are kept in the temple, or 'god house'.

The State of Veracruz is extraordinarily rich in pottery, yet its produce is rarely seen beyond the locality where it is made. In the Totonac communities which surround Papantla, cooking utensils and incense burners, some shaped like birds, are made for family use in large numbers of houses by women who rely on nearby clay deposits. Sometimes objects are fired indoors in the embers of the cooking stove. A rapidly diminishing supply of firewood – the result of deforestation – now threatens this ancient tradition. Pesticides have also reduced the meagre population of native, stingless bees. Reared by families in communities such as Cerro del Carbón, they live in pottery beehives on wooden shelves fixed to the front of houses.

Potters in communities such as these need little by way of equipment. After it has been excavated and transported home, clay is sun-dried and laboriously

Small pre-Hispanic polychrome bowl of the Late Post-Classic period, belonging to the Mixtec culture. Found in Zaachila, Oaxaca, it features a bright blue humming bird perched on the rim. H of bowl rim 2⅛" (5.4 cm).

ground. Sometimes it is passed through wire mesh. Next the clay is mixed with water until it achieves a proper consistency, and kneaded by hand or trampled with bare feet. It is then kept under a plastic sheet or stored underground in a hole until needed. As in pre-Hispanic times vessels are often fashioned without a potter's wheel.

Amatenango del Valle, in the State of Chiapas, provides neighbouring communities with water storage jars, pots, dishes and toys (pls 68, 116). Large pots are built up by women over several days from long tubes of clay which are coiled around and pressed down with the fingers. Because shade and coolness are necessary if the clay is to remain moist, many women prefer to work indoors. Some choose to sit outside, however, under overhanging thatched eaves, and to suspend a blanket for extra protection against the sun's rays.

Many potters in Amatenango del Valle use a rotating device. Half-finished vessels are placed on a wooden board, which rests on a stone or inverted bowl. This enables women to remain seated on the ground, and to turn pots as they fashion the walls. Left to harden, pots are burnished with a dry stone. Here, as in many other villages, pottery may be given a slip of rusty orange or ivory-coloured liquid clay. A twig, a feather, a homemade brush or a finger serves to paint on the snake-like lines, flowers and leaf motifs that adorn finished vessels. Colours for painting are made by dissolving locally found earths with water in the hollow of a stone. Before being fired, pieces are set out in the sunshine; otherwise they would crack in the heat of the flames. When they are warm, they are carefully stacked in the yard or out on the public highway. Covered with a mound of wood, cow dung and maize husks, they are fired for around thirty minutes.

Ancient production methods are still favoured by the Zapotec of San Bartolo Coyotepec in Oaxaca. Here pots begin as lumps of dark clay which are hollowed out with the fist; walls are built up from the inside with more clay, and smoothed with a piece of broken pottery. Wet leather is used to create a flaring lip. A dish, upturned on a second dish, supports the pot and enables it to spin at up to ninety revolutions per minute. If women want to pattern vessels, they can polish them in sections, scratch motifs with a nail, or perforate the clay.

San Bartolo Coyotepec is famous for the black and brilliant sheen of its pottery (pl. 70). This is the result of overnight firing in a reducing atmosphere. The kiln, circular in form, lies in a pit with its opening at ground level; because the clay is starved of oxygen, the red iron oxide is reduced to black iron oxide. The next day, friction with a rag removes the grime and reveals the black metallic lustre of polished areas; unpolished areas are gunmetal grey.

Not all traditional pottery is modelled by hand. Moulds were frequently employed in pre-Conquest times, and today their use is widespread in Indian Mexico. With this method flat sheets of clay are pressed into or over the mould with the fingers; a sprinkling of ashes or white dust prevents the clay from sticking. Obvious joins or roughness are eliminated with the palm of the hand, or with a cloth, maize cob or polishing stone. Complex forms may be partially mould-made, but completed by hand. This is true of zoomorphic jugs used to carry holy water from the spring of Our Lady of Ocotlán in Tlaxcala. The mould-made base is finished off with the head of an antlered deer or long-necked duck. Jugs are given an orange slip, burnished, then incised with flower and leaf designs (pl. 65). In addition to the decorative methods already mentioned, surfaces may be stamped with repeat patterning or embellished in high-relief. Some techniques are strictly regional. Near Tantoyuca, Veracruz, Huastec women anoint burnished pots with maize water; during firing, surfaces acquire a dappled appearance where heat has partially scorched the clay.

Pre-Hispanic Maya polychrome vessel with glyph panels, showing male figures with voluminous head-dresses and ornaments for the ear, wrist and neck.

Human figurines reminiscent of pre-Hispanic examples are modelled in many places, although themes often belong to the twentieth century. Recently made pieces from San Miguel Aguasuelos in Veracruz include a woman on horseback, a man ploughing a field, a game of cards, and an aeroplane with passengers. Atzompa in Oaxaca is famed for the creation of *muñecas bordadas* (embroidered dolls). Initiated by the late Teodora Blanca, these terracotta figurines wear dresses with raised flower designs, and carry birds or baskets on their heads. Other hand-modelled pieces from Atzompa may be less ornate; one potter chose recently to show the local jail, with wives bringing baskets of food to prisoners behind barred windows. Sometimes figurines are made for ceremonial occasions. In the Vishana area of Tehuantepec, Oaxaca, clay women are given out on 6 January (Day of the Three Kings). Painted with slashes of white and gold, they combine mould-made and hand-modelled elements.

Contemporary potters do not draw solely on their pre-Conquest heritage, however. The impact of Spanish technology was widely felt in most regions. Makeshift kick wheels, ingeniously constructed by their users, have been adopted by male potters in innumerable centres, while enclosed kilns have largely replaced pre-Hispanic firing methods. Although resinless wood remains the most common fuel, kerosine is a popular alternative. Introduced forms, such as the candlestick, have also become established; today they feature in the output of countless potters.

The fusion of Old and New World traditions is excellently demonstrated by the work of Herón Martínez Mendoza. Born in 1918 in Acatlán, Puebla, this remarkable craftsman began his career making pots and water jars in the local style. Since then he has dedicated himself to the creation of new and ever more elaborate forms. Hand-modelled, burnished and adorned with earth markings, Herón's pieces show extraordinary skill and imagination (pl. 63). Zoomorphic pots, pyramids of animals, and tall candelabra incorporating foliage, deer, mermaids and moons are fired in large kilns with cactus spikes and other fuel.

Glazing requires pottery to be fired twice. Since its introduction it has become a functional and decorative element in both cities and villages. Low-priced dishes, pots and mugs which gleam in the sunlight are displayed in markets everywhere. A transparent lead glaze is the type most often used. In the State of Michoacán potters from Capula now paint tea and dinner sets with geometric patterning, flowers, animals and fish; dishes from Tzintzuntzan display fishing boats and regionally dressed women carrying baskets or flowers. The famous *petatillo* ware of Tonalá in Jalisco is distinguished by a profusion of animals, birds, ferns and flowers on a delicately cross-hatched background. Humorous verses and sayings adorn pitchers and *pulque* mugs from Tecomatepec in the State of Mexico. 'Women are devils when they wish to wed', warns one; 'Let him who empties me, fill me' advises another. Spirited scenes often accompany these messages: tigers stalk deer or fight among themselves, well protected by the clear glaze which covers them.

Black glazes and amber-coloured glazes with cadmium are popular in many regions (pl. 69). Green glazes with copper oxide are especially common in Michoacán. Potters from Patamban produce punch bowls and tableware with birds, animals and curling ferns; painted in white, these motifs show bright green under the glaze. San José de Gracia has become famous in recent years for its gigantic pineapple-shaped vessels, wholly covered with spines and mould-made leaves. In the city of Oaxaca, drip glazing with a variety of colours gives kitchenware a cheerful, rainbow appearance.

Although the amount of poison that can be dissolved from such pottery is small, visitors to Mexico from Europe and the USA are often nervous about using lead-glazed vessels. David Barkin shares their concern. Currently working outside the Government for the *Dirección de Ecodesarollo* (Commission for Ecodevelopment), he is making a study of cooking methods in Michoacán and developing an educational campaign. Because present-day glazes are often under-fired, they are vulnerable to the acids contained in lemon juice, tomatoes or coffee. His aim is to change firing techniques by raising temperatures. Where lead glazes have been fully fused, there is little to fear.

Tin glazing is essential to the art of maiolica. In Colonial times the most important tin-glazed earthenware was made in Puebla city. Known as *Talavera*, because it resembled pottery from Talavera de la Reina in Spain, it was distributed throughout Mexico and beyond. Production methods were regulated by ordinances. In and around Puebla city the façades of seventeenth- and eighteenth-century churches and houses were magnificently decorated with gleaming tiles; pharmacies were lined with *Talavera* jars; kitchens in convents and private homes were tiled and decked out with a profusion of tableware. Styles show a combination of Islamic, Spanish, Italian, Chinese and indigenous traits. Despite a decline during the early nineteenth century, the art of *Talavera* is still practised

in Puebla. Methods and materials have changed very little since the sixteenth century. Potters use two kinds of clay; sifted for impurities, they are mixed and soaked in water tanks. Shaping is done on the wheel. Pieces are given a soft firing, covered with an opaque, white glaze made from tin and lead, then decorated with mineral colours. During the second firing, at temperatures of around 1000°C, the colouring oxides sink into and stain the glaze, producing inglaze decoration. Fine maiolica was similarly produced in the town of Guanajuato, where the art has been revived in recent years by Gorki González, who even studied Oriental techniques in Japan to further improve his skills.

Oriental influence also underlies Mexico's most recent and resistant type of pottery. Stoneware, fired at temperatures above 1200°C, has been produced for the past thirty-five years in the small town of Tonalá in Jalisco by the renowned ceramist Jorge Wilmot. Dinner sets and more traditional forms are painted with a subtle range of colours and an economy of design (pl. 72). Often exported, this type of stoneware is also popular with wealthier families in towns.

Factory paints and other modern preparations have been adopted in recent decades for the creation of much ornamental pottery. Figurines made today in San Pedro Tlaquepaque, Jalisco, are usually decorated with gloss paints, or sprayed from aerosol cans. Guadalupe Panduro is one of very few remaining potters who still fix aniline powders with a Mexican resin similar to gum arabic. Now in his eighties, this superb craftsman is known for his *tipos*, or genre figurines. Made partly by mould and partly by hand, they portray presidents, dandies, musicians, horsemen and market-vendors, which conjure up the vanished world of nineteenth-century *costumbrista* paintings (pl. 78).

Twentieth-century customs, seasoned liberally with fantasy, inspired the work of the late Candelario Medrano. Born in Santa Cruz de las Huertas,

Mould-made pots for piñatas *in the State of Mexico.*

Jalisco, he developed a highly personal and instantly recognizable style. Churches with miniature human figures hanging out of belfry windows, aeroplanes, Noah's Arks bedecked with Mexican flags, masked dancers and village bandstands were included in his prolific output (pl. 77). Together with the lions, roosters and surreal creatures which he also liked to produce, they were painted with aniline colours and varnished. His work, like that of Teodora Blanco, has attracted imitators who are now referred to as 'school of . . .' by commentators.

Candelario Medrano's inventiveness grew out of toy-making. The same is true for Purépecha potters in San Pedro Ocumicho, Michoacán (pls 74, 75, 115). An upsurge of creativity in recent years has made this one of the most famous villages in Mexico. Although the elaboration of whistles and money-banks has traditionally been the work of women, it was a male ceramist who initiated a remarkable change of direction. Marcelino Vicente, killed in a drunken brawl in 1968 at the age of thirty-five, inspired the women of Ocumicho to widen their range of expression. In her publication entitled *Ocumicho*, Louisa Reynoso has charted the various phases of production. Early, often grotesque, pieces featuring devils were later joined by suns, moons, skeletons and mermaids. By the late 1970s humour had become a strong element: devils were shown riding motorcycles, learning to read in school or playing football. A recent trend has been towards erotic tableaux which have a market in the USA.

Ocumicho is benefiting from the growth of a new buying public. Serious collectors and casual purchasers, both at home and abroad, now support a wide range of non-functional Mexican crafts. Women in Ocumicho give free rein to their imaginations; as a result no two pieces are ever completely alike.

The introduction of Christian themes was a significant factor in the evolution of Mexican pottery. After the Conquest representations of native gods were supplanted by images of Virgins, saints, devils and angels. Today such figures adorn candelabra in the town of Izúcar de Matamoros, Puebla. These often elaborate structures are modelled by hand, and hung with a multitude of tiny moulded birds, fruits or flowers on wires. According to Marian Harvey, candelabra featuring Adam and Eve were formerly commissioned for local weddings; incense-burners representing the twelve apostles were carried in religious processions on the feast day of Saint Peter and Saint Paul. Today pieces are mostly made for sale to outsiders by two families. Aurelio Flores died recently, to the sorrow of his many admirers. Although his sons seem likely to continue working, pottery production is currently dominated by the Castillo family. Huge candelabra depicting the Nativity, the Garden of Eden or the Day of the Dead are fashioned and painted with exquisite refinement by Alfonso Castillo, while his brother Heriberto creates witty and brilliantly coloured figures (pls 15, 62).

In Metepec, by contrast, the makers of pottery are legion. Situated less than fifty kilometres from Mexico City, this small town is renowned for the scale and flamboyance of its production. Winged horses, guitar-playing mermaids and regally crowned lions abound (pls 79, 112). Sometimes the façades of houses are adorned with clay suns, moons and angels. Not content with decorating just the outside of his house, Adrián Luis González has also fashioned elaborate bed-heads, mirror frames and wall-plaques for the enjoyment of his family.

Several potters, like Alfonso Soteno, specialize in gigantic candelabra known as 'trees of life'. Thought to have originated in the Middle East, this important symbol came to acquire a Judeo-Christian meaning. Trees of Life in Metepec portray the Fall of Man: Adam and Eve, clad in fig-leaves, give way to temptation in the Garden of Eden. Local church imagery and the Old Testament provide Tiburcio Soteno with a seemingly endless source of inspiration. Archangels, devils and saints proliferate in his work; one prize-winning piece in honour of the Virgin of Guadalupe was even sent to the Vatican. Metepec is also open to modern trends, however. After the Olympics of 1968 various customers apparently ordered 'Olympic' trees; in 1989 Oscar Soteno peopled several trees of life with characters from 'Batman'. Vibrant commercial paints and gilding are preferred by many potters; others have recently opted for a sombre style which they term '*barroco*' (baroque).

Contemporary Mexican ceramics range, as they did before the Conquest, from simple elegance to profuse ornamentation. In some centres contemporary potters adhere closely to tradition and anonymity; in others they seek innovation and self-expression. Often using the simplest of tools and relying on instinct rather than science, the men and women mentioned in this chapter have one thing in common: their creations, whether functional, ceremonial or purely decorative, are all worked with loving care. It is their very fragility which lends them such charm and fascination.

63 RIGHT *Cow, with adjoining calves and candle supports, by Herón Martínez of Acatlán, Puebla. Surfaces have been given an orange slip and burnished. Zoomorphic forms have a long history in Mexico. H 17⅜" (44 cm).*

64 *Hand-modelled clay animals, fired without a kiln, from the Lacandón community of Najá, Chiapas. L of reptile 12¾" (32.5 cm).*

65 RIGHT *Duck-shaped vessel with an orange slip from Ocotlán, Tlaxcala. Surfaces are burnished, and decoration is incised. H 14¼" (36 cm).*

67 BELOW *Lacandón armadillo from Najá, Chiapas. L 7" (18 cm).*

68 BOTTOM *Burnished pot, with an ivory-coloured slip and raised designs, from the Tzeltal village of Amatenango del Valle, Chiapas. Fired without a kiln, it has been painted with earth colours. H 9⅞" (25 cm).*

66 ABOVE *Hand-modelled clay figure, with some earth colouring, from Santa María Tetecla, Veracruz. Such figures are made for the Festival of the Dead. H 6¾" (17 cm).*

69 LEFT *Black-glazed candelabrum with five candle-supports; the lid is patterned with perforations. Pottery of this type is made in the Purépecha village of Santa Fé de la Laguna, Michoacán, for the Festival of the Dead. H 15¾" (40 cm).*

70 RIGHT *Burnished black Zapotec pot, fired in a reducing atmosphere, from San Bartolo Coyotepec, Oaxaca. H 14" (35.5 cm).*

71 BELOW *Maiolica pot and lid from Dolores Hidalgo, Guanajuato. This town was a major centre for maiolica throughout the nineteenth century. H 15" (38 cm).*

72 ABOVE RIGHT *Stoneware dish by Jorge Wilmot of Tonalá, Jalisco. Painted designs show pre-Hispanic inspiration. D approx. 13" (33 cm).*

73 RIGHT *Maiolica dish from the workshop of Gorki González, Guanajuato. D 12⅝" (32 cm).*

75 BELOW *Motorcyclist with skull from Ocumicho, Michoacán. H 10⅝" (27 cm).*

76 BOTTOM *Adam and Eve, decorated with commercial paints and varnished, from Izúcar de Matamoros, Puebla. H 8" (20.5 cm).*

74 BELOW *A vision of hell, hand-modelled and decorated with commercial paints by María de Jesus Candelaria, from the Purépecha village of Ocumicho, Michoacán. H 16⅛" (41 cm).*

78 BELOW *Pot-seller of painted clay, with dried moss; hand- and mould-made by Guadalupe Panduro from San Pedro Tlaquepaque, Jalisco. H 4⅜" (11 cm).*

79 BOTTOM *Winged horses from Metepec, State of Mexico. Made from old moulds, they are exuberantly decorated with commercially produced paints. H 18¼" (46.5 cm).*

77 ABOVE *Bandstand with musicians and dancers, hand- and mould-made by Candelario Medrano from Santa Cruz de las Huertas, Jalisco. Figures are supported by wires. H 22" (56 cm).*

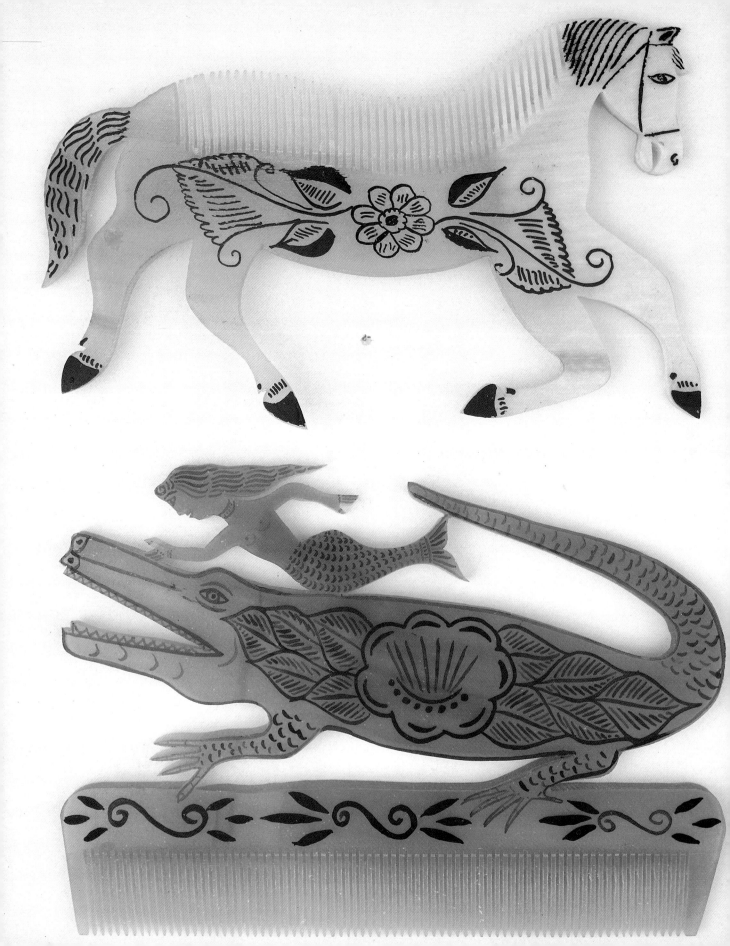

CHAPTER V

AN ABUNDANCE OF CRAFTS

THERE IS HARDLY A SUBSTANCE in Mexico that is not made to serve a functional, ceremonial or decorative purpose. Plant fibres and other vegetable materials have long been a part of life. Among the artefacts left by seasonally nomadic hunters in the rock ̇helters of Tamaulipas and the Tehuacán Valley were the remains of cordage, twining and netting. These have been dated to between 6500 BC and 2000 BC. Twilled mats were also present. Known as *petates* and made from palm or rushes, they are still used in large areas of Indian Mexico for sitting and sleeping, or for transporting flowers and other produce. Babies are born on *petates* and the dead are buried in them.

This sort of continuity is also true of basketry skills, which anticipated pottery and textile weaving by several thousand years. Today baskets remain a major necessity, with different regions favouring local materials. One extremely popular method relies on the interweaving at right angles of palm or rush strips. In Santa María Chigmecatitlán, Puebla, and in parts of Oaxaca undyed palm is combined with dark or aniline-coloured strands to create complex geometric designs. Twilled baskets with double walls and bottoms are fashioned with enormous skill from local plant species by the Tarahumara Indians of Chihuahua.

Coiling is also practised in several regions. During basket-making multi-coloured palm strips are wrapped round a foundation of grasses. In Santa Ana Tepaltitlán in the State of Mexico the resulting tubes are widely spaced; patterns include zigzag lines, stars and butterflies. By contrast the baskets of Seri Indians in Sonora are compactly coiled to hold liquids as well as dry substances. Made from light and dark fibres which expand when damp, they feature geometric designs and recall south-western basketry styles from the USA. Further systems of construction employ the principles of twining and wickerwork. Flamboyant palm baskets from Guerrero are patterned with pink horses, purple squirrels and brightly dressed women. Willow, cane, bamboo, wheatstraw and agave fibres are just some of many materials that also lend themselves to the creation of beautiful yet sturdy baskets.

When Aztec emissaries first saw the round hats of the *conquistadores*, they likened them to small *comales*, or clay griddles. Today hats are an essential feature of Mexican male attire, despite strong competition in recent years from baseball caps. Shapes vary according to region; nowhere, however, are brims as broad or crowns as high as they were at the turn of the century. The finest hats

80 LEFT *Horn combs, with painted decoration, from San Antonio de la Isla, State of Mexico. Horse 3⅛" x 5¼" (8 x 13.2 cm). Alligator with mermaid 3¾" x 5¼" (9.5 x 13.2 cm).*

are reputed to come from Becal in Campeche. Called *jipi* hats and made from *jipijapa*, a palm-like species known to botanists as *Carludovica palmata*, they are fashioned in caves where the cool, damp atmosphere prevents the leaves from becoming brittle. In other regions less rarefied palm species are worked outdoors. Men, women and children in parts of Guerrero and Oaxaca even braid palm strips while walking.

Large quantities of braided palm are bought by semi-industrialized hat-making centres in towns, but numerous Indian groups continue to assemble their own hats, sewing the flattened strips to shape by hand or even by machine. Predictably the greatest diversity lies with home-made examples. Among the Huichol hats are decorated with iridescent plumes, double-woven ribbons or beaded bands, and hung with flannel crosses, bead droplets, colourful woollen pompons, seed pods, *madroño* leaves, squirrel tails and even metal rings from the lids of beer cans.

The preparation of agave fibres has been described in Chapter II. When spun, they are often woven into shoulder-bags (pl. 46). Hard-wearing netted bags, which expand the more they have to carry, are produced in several states. The ancient skill of netting also serves to create elaborately patterned henequen hammocks. Throughout the State of Yucatán these are widely used for sleeping, although it seems certain that hammocks were introduced by the Spaniards from the Caribbean region.

Markets remain the normal outlet for most wares. Spread out on the ground are *tortilla* baskets, fans for the fire, bunches of twigs for scouring plates, brushes, brooms and lengths of rope. Wicker cradles and baskets in the shape of owls and chickens are produced in Tequisquiapan, Querétaro, and sold in San Juan del Río. Still more imaginative are ornamental cane birdcages from the State of Hidalgo. Topped with splendid turrets and domes, they stand more than 2′4″ (70 cm) high. Not far from Mexico City craftsmen near Lerma specialize in making rush chairs and stools; on Sundays motorists entering the capital by certain roads are likely to see impromptu furniture stores set up on grass verges.

The skills described above afford a living to many thousands of people in Mexico, where every community knows how best to use the natural resources at its disposal. Of the many vegetable substances which are still worked one of the strangest must surely be gum, or *chilte*. Extracted as a milky liquid from forest trees in Jalisco, Tabasco and Quintana Roo, it is brightly coloured with aniline and vegetable dyes. Creations, which are sold during religious festivals, include diminutive figures of the Virgin Mary, churches, shoes, lace-like baskets of fruit and flowers, fountains and miniature gardens. Near Papantla in the State of Veracruz, sun-dried vanilla pods are also fashioned into a multitude of forms, such as flowers, hearts and figures of Christ. Before the arrival of oil wells and petrol fumes, this fragrant plant used to scent the autumn air.

Selection of hats in a country market. In rural areas palm hats are still an essential feature of male attire.

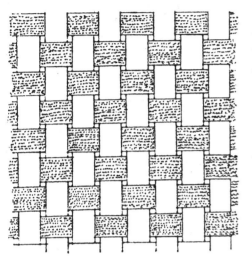

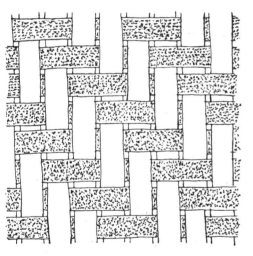

Mat-making. This technique, also used for baskets and hats, requires two elements to cross at right angles. Both are equally active. The top example is checker-woven on an over-one-under-one principle, while the other is twill-woven to create diagonal patterning.

Cloth, made from the beaten inner bark of Moraceae trees, provided articles of clothing and adornment in pre-Hispanic times. Its survival among the contemporary Lacandón of Najá has been described in Chapter II. Bark paper, or *amate*, has a smoother texture. Today the art of paper-making persists in the borderline area where the states of Puebla, Hidalgo and Veracruz meet. There bark paper serves as a magic ingredient in various non-Christian rites. The Otomí Indians of San Pablito use two kinds of tree. The mulberry (*Morus*), known locally as *moral*, gives a whitish paper; the fig (*Ficus*), known locally as *xalama*, gives a dark paper. After the bark has been peeled from trees by male villagers, it can be dried and stored for future use. Women are responsible for the making of paper. First the bark is washed, then it is boiled in a cauldron for several hours with ashes or the lime water used to cook maize. After rinsing, the fibres are laid in lines on a wooden board and beaten with a stone until they fuse together; boards remain in the sun until the paper dries. The ceremonial uses of bark paper in San Pablito are described in Chapter VII. Outside demand is now such, however, that trees are being over-stripped. The poaching of bark from neighbours' trees, often before they are fully grown, has become a frequent problem. Requests for light paper have led to a severe shortage, and darker papers are often bleached.

Much of this paper is now destined for Xalitla, Ameyaltepec and other Nahua villages in Guerrero. Here men and women, who once dedicated themselves to decorating pottery, paint colourful landscapes which combine fantasy with realism. According to the artist Felipe Ehrenberg, this trend began in 1961 in Ameyaltepec. Potters in the area were regularly transporting their wares by mule along unpaved tracks to the highway, and accepting the high number of breakages as inevitable. Felipe Ehrenberg and a colleague encouraged them to paint on *amate*; other villages followed suit, and a substantial market now exists for this work.

Before the Conquest codices, or pictorial manuscripts, were painted on deerskin, bark paper, or more rarely agave paper. Themes included astrology, history, prophesy and ritual; gods, priests, rulers and warriors were shown in profile and outlined in black, usually against a gesso background. Modern bark paintings recall this vanished skill. Although airports and souvenir shops offer an endless supply of inferior paintings from Guerrero, the best constitute a rich and valuable source of information about contemporary village life. The subjects, often shown in profile, are the villagers themselves, engaged in ploughing, fishing and harvesting, or attending church masses and festivals. A few villagers in San Pablito, inspired by the success of those who purchase their paper, have in turn adopted picture painting as a craft. In 1984 a local artist, Rafael Lechuga, was commissioned by I.N.E.A. (a government organization for adult education) to give painting classes in San Pablito. Whereas the majority of these ex-students merely imitate inferior work from Guerrero, one painter has forged his own style. Using Otomí designs from embroidered garments and incorporating the deities traditionally represented by bark papercuts, Rosendo Calisto produces brilliantly coloured non-narrative pictures which feature interlocking figures and symbols.

In the Aztec realm of Anáhuac feather-workers commanded great respect. Like goldsmiths and lapidaries, they belonged to guilds and inhabited a special quarter of the capital. Although few examples of their work survive, we know that the shields and capes of warriors were often decorated with figurative designs; feathers were fastened to backgrounds with paste, or attached by needle and thread. After the Conquest Christian images and *costumbrista* themes were sometimes rendered in feathers. Today, however, the art is limited to greetings cards and to the feathered shields of performers during *La Danza de los Concheros*. With their ornate costumes, they remind spectators of Aztec splendour from a vanished era. The pictorial art of *popote*, popular during the 1920s and 30s, is still practised in and around Mexico City by a few dedicated craftsmen. Like feather-workers, they construct a mosaic: tiny aniline-coloured straws, pressed down one by one on to wax-covered boards, form religious images and scenes from a pre-industrial age (pl. 83).

Gourds have a long history in Mexico. In the north-east the bottle gourd, *Lagenaria siceraria*, had already been domesticated by about 6500 BC. In countless regions this natural container is still used for water and other liquids; often a maize cob serves as a stopper. The rind of fruit from the calabash tree, *Crescentia cujete*, provides country dwellers with bowls for food and drink. Writing soon after the Conquest, Bernal Díaz del Castillo described how beautiful girls brought deep gourd basins to the Aztec emperor, so that he could wash his hands before eating. In contemporary Mexico these all-purpose vessels are also perforated for use as strainers, employed as receptacles for tools and small objects, adapted to serve as musical instruments, or worn on the head as protection against the sun's rays. In Pinotepa de Don Luis, Oaxaca, and in parts of Tabasco, gourds are decoratively incised by the Mixtec and the Chontal (pl. 90). The most widely admired form of decoration, however, is provided by lacquer-workers in the states of Guerrero, Michoacán and Chiapas. Ingredients and methods may vary, but all concerned agree that work is slow and laborious. Archaeological remains and references by Spanish chroniclers confirm the existence of this art in pre-Conquest times.

Acapetlahuaya, set deep in a valley and surrounded on all sides by the rolling hills of Guerrero, retains the use of lacquered vessels (pl. 89). Left to dry out, gourds are later cut down the middle and placed in water until the insides rot; the hard rind is then cleaned out and smoothed. Ingredients are finely ground by hand. When inner surfaces have been smeared with oil from the toasted seeds of

Ancient Mixtec warrior from the Codex Nuttall, which was painted on screen-folded strips of gesso-coated deerskin. Characters, often richly attired and brightly coloured, were shown in profile, according to the conventions of the period.

chía (*Salvia hispanica*), they are lined with powdered brown earth. Next follow two coats of paste; this is made from a ground white mineral mixed with water and red commercial pigment. Operations are spread over several days. When the last layer has hardened, flower, bird and animal motifs are painted on; a final coating of oil seals the lacquer, making it heat- and water-resistant. Gourds in Acapetlahuaya are used for *atole* – a hot pre-Hispanic drink. According to Efrain Martínez Zuluaga, 'It doesn't taste the same in clay or plastic. Long ago we sent decorated gourds as tribute to the Aztec capital, and we use them still. Yet few of us now know how to do this work. It is hard and demanding; often my hands are rubbed raw. What modern man would want to do my job?' Despite his words, however, this wise and knowledgeable craftsman is proud of his calling and sad that the young apparently care little for village traditions.

There is no shortage of lacquer-workers in Olinalá. Not just gourds but trays, dishes, boxes and trunks made from pine and sweet-smelling *linaloé* wood are lavishly decorated by men, women and even children. Layer by layer, a resistant coat of lacquer is built up, left to harden and polished with a soft cloth. Wares are painted with a profusion of flowers, foliage, birds and popular sayings (pl. 94). Francisco Colonel also specializes in working with gold leaf, achieving dazzling and magical results. A second decorative method which has brought fame to Olinalá is the art of *rayado*. With this ingenious technique surfaces are given two coats of lacquer in contrasting colours. When designs have been scratched with a thorn or needle, the top coat is partially scraped away. High-relief birds, butterflies, leaping deer and geometric borders are recurrent motifs. Styles are never static, and innovations are quickly copied; not long ago several artisans decided to pattern their wares in a *pointilliste* manner using a variety of colours. Because lacquers from Olinalá are damaged by moisture, a few producers have recently started to varnish their wares, thereby giving them an unpleasantly shiny appearance like plastic.

If awards were ever given out for enterprise, however, they should go to lacquer-workers in nearby Temalacacingo. Driven by the need to expand their market, they search ceaselessly for new and eye-catching forms. Execution methods may be rougher than those of their neighbours, but innovation and wit are key factors. Decorative masks, gourd handbags and crosses, together with a succession of ornaments and toys, are sold at fairs and markets everywhere; the constant quest for novelty even led one family to lacquer empty sardine cans. Unfortunately many workers have begun to rely almost exclusively on gloss paints; cheerfully decorated, waterproof gourds are now used in many regions for serving frothy chocolate and other drinks.

In Chiapa de Corzo, Chiapas, powders are fixed not with oil but with *aje* – a greasy, yellowish substance obtained from tiny tree-parasites (*Coccus axin*). Reared in Venustiano Carranza, adult insects are boiled, crushed and sieved

Aztec feather-worker from the Codex Florentino, also entitled General History of the Things of New Spain. *Compiled soon after the Conquest by Fray Bernardino de Sahagún, this invaluable work described the techniques used by feather-workers. One method consisted in 'fastening the feathers to the background with paste', while a second required the additional aid of 'thread and cord'.*

through cloth; the resulting fat is beaten until it sets, then stored in maize husks. Men in Chiapa de Corzo clean gourds and construct wooden boxes. Women like Luvia Macías de Blanco use home-made cats' hair brushes to paint lacquered surfaces with floral designs, often blending colours together with the fingertips. Lacquered gourds from Chiapa de Corzo are traditionally bought by Zapotec women from the Isthmus of Tehuantepec; filled with fruit and sweets, they are carried on the head during religious festivals.

The elaborate task of *embutido*, or incrustation, is carried out in Uruapan, Michoacán. Gourds and large trays of resinless wood are lacquered in a single colour with the help of *aje*. Designs are excised with a sharp instrument and the hollows filled in with different colours; lighter shades of lacquer are inlaid last. Crescent moons, birds, animals and human figures predominate, accompanied always by a profusion of flowers. There are various theories which consider possible foreign influences on work from these different centres. It is generally agreed, however, that styles in Pátzcuaro were affected during the Colonial period by lacquered wares imported from Asia. Today gourds and trays carry exotic scenes featuring birds, animals and luxuriant plants. These are painted with imported oil colours and embellished with gold leaf.

Wood has many uses other than those described above. Up and down the country, in large towns and small hamlets, it is worked in an infinity of ways: no market is complete without an array of spoons and chocolate whisks. Popular wares include orangewood combs from Oaxaca, duck- and swan-shaped vessels from Ixtapan de la Sal, furniture carved in Cuanajo with flowers, birds and angels, inlaid boxes from Santa María del Río, resonant guitars from Paracho and brightly painted animals from Arrasola and San Martín Tilcajete. These have little in common with the highly stylized and richly polished figures of the Seri Indians. Drawing their inspiration from nature, they use *palo fierro* (literally, ironwood) to create powerful dolphins, turtles and deadly stingrays.

Mexican carvers have long worked with a further range of materials. Stone tools and vessels were plentiful in the earliest of settlements. Later civilizations excelled as builders and sculptors. Today grinding stones are used, as they were in pre-Hispanic times, for the preparation of food; from San Salvador el Seco in Puebla come mortars hewn in the shape of animals. In the same state the inhabitants of Tecali convert blocks of onyx into handsome vases, boxes, goblets and ornamental bowls of coloured fruit.

Bone also has a long history; jaguar bones, carved with historic and mythological scenes, are among ancient Mixtec treasures discovered by archaeologists at Monte Albán, Oaxaca. One of Mexico's finest craftsmen, Roberto Ruiz, has been carving bone for most of his life. Born in Oaxaca, he now lives on the outskirts of Mexico City, and devotes himself almost exclusively to the miniature and to the theme of death (pls 104, 105). He describes his work as 'a sort of

Tzotzil Indian from Zinacantán, Chiapas, with strips of palm. He wears a candy-striped, home-woven cotton colera, *or tunic, and a home-made palm hat. In this community hats are often adorned with brightly coloured ribbons.*

labyrinth. I am an embroiderer in bone; my figures emerge as I work and continually surprise me. I have to scrape away the bone to see what lies within.' With his dentist's drill, don Roberto achieves work as delicate as filigree. Revolutionaries, weavers, typists and musicians are all shown as diminutive skeletons in the midst of their everyday activities. This is in the tradition of Guadalupe Posada, whose engravings are a constant source of inspiration.

Metalworking remains one of the most important crafts in Mexico. As described in Chapter III, gold- and silversmiths still excel at making jewelry and other adornments. Copper is the speciality of craftsmen in Santa Clara del Cobre, Michoacán. Here the rhythmic sound of hammering echoes through the town as lumps of molten metal, red hot from the fire, are stretched and beaten on the anvil to become cauldrons, jugs or dishes, often embossed with elaborate designs. Wrought iron, used throughout the Colonial period for gates, windows, balustrades and weather vanes, was introduced from Spain. Today the art has degenerated, although beautiful hand-forged crosses, replete with suns and moons, adorn houses in San Cristóbal de las Casas, Chiapas.

European technology is also responsible for steel tools; these are currently produced in several regions. Horn-handled *machetes* from Oaxaca are engraved with acid to display lively scenes and well-known mottoes. Amid mountains and fleeing deer we read: 'He who keeps company with wolves learns to howl', or 'Faces we see, hearts we can never know'. Because tin is light and flexible, it is worked in a number of highly decorative ways. In the city of Oaxaca thin sheets are cut out with shears, embossed, soldered, left plain or painted with bright, translucent colours. To enter the homes of Aarón and José Velasco is to encounter a world of gleaming suns, parrots, ships, angels and ornamental trees full of birds and fruit (pls 1, 106).

After the Conquest Spanish methods for treating leather were introduced, together with skills involving European materials such as glass and paper. They too have become a focus for Mexican creativity. Paper is the tool of the Linares family in Mexico City. From making traditional papier mâché toys Pedro Linares extended his range to include *alebrijes*. These imaginatively painted fairy-tale monsters, which encompass dragons with forked tongues, two-headed creatures and winged fish on legs, are now made by his son Felipe and by Felipe's sons. In their cramped rooftop workroom, hung with unfinished limbs and a paper television set, three Linares generations strive to meet a never-ending stream of additional orders for skeletons and skulls with flower-painted eye sockets (pls 108, 109). Working with paper and wire, Saulo Moreno has also forged a unique style (pl. 110). Red-painted devils, skeletons, mermaids and strange animals deploy the wit and ingenuity of this erstwhile painter, and render meaningless the distinction between craft and art.

Wrought ironwork was a notable architectural feature in Puebla and other Colonial cities. These examples, from the Museo Bello, show highly decorated key-holes. The double-headed eagle, emblem of the house of Habsburg, was a popular design with iron-workers.

81 *Coiled basket, featuring dyed palm strands*
wrapped round grasses, from Santa Ana
Tepaltitlán, State of Mexico. D 10½" (26.5 cm).

82 BELOW LEFT *Baskets of interwoven palm strands, dyed and undyed, from the Mixtec area of Oaxaca. H of tallest 11" (28 cm).*

83 BELOW RIGHT *The art of* popote *has been used to show the Virgin of Guadalupe; with this technique dyed straws are stuck down one by one. 6½" x 12⅜" (16.5 x 31.5 cm).*

84 *Scorpions of plaited vanilla, with glass beads for eyes, from Papantla, Veracruz. L approx.* *5½" (14 cm).*

85 Cut-out designs of dark bark paper on a light bark paper background, from the Otomí village of San Pablito, Puebla. Inspired by traditional bark figures representing seed spirits, this example was made for sale to outsiders. 22¾" x 15¼" (57.8 x 38.7 cm).

86 Picture painted on bark paper in the Nahua village of Ameyaltepec, Guerrero. The artist, Felix Venancio, portrays daily life in his village. 15¾" x 11⅜" (40 x 29 cm).

87, 88 Pictures painted on bark paper in Ameyaltepec, Guerrero. The artist, Miguel Ascencio, shows a local festival. OPPOSITE, ABOVE By day dancers and musicians gather outside the church. OPPOSITE, BELOW At night children break a piñata. 11⅜" x 16⅛" (29 x 41 cm).

89 *Lacquered gourd painted by Efraín Martínez Zuluaga and his sons in Acapetlahuaya, Guerrero. It shows the Aztec emperor Cuauhtemoc blowing the conch for war atop a pyramid. D 11¼" (28.5 cm).*

90 Decoratively incised gourds and gourd
rattles from the Mixtec village of Pinotepa de
Don Luis, Oaxaca. D of largest gourd approx.
6⅞" (17.5 cm).

91, 92, 93 Lacquerwork with painted designs from
Olinalá, Guerrero. BELOW Wooden tray. 20⅛″ x 14⅛″
(51.3 x 36 cm). BELOW RIGHT Gourd, cut into two
sections, with a wooden bird. H 10⅜″ (26.5 cm).
BOTTOM RIGHT Wooden box, painted with tiger motifs
by Francisco Colonel. Lid 3½″ x 4⅜″ (8.8 x 11 cm).

94 *Lacquered wooden box from Olinalá, Guerrero. Painted by Juan García, it carries the following message, conveyed in words and images: 'When love unites two faithful hearts, one key secures them and one lance protects them.' Lid 4" x 7½" (10 x 19 cm).*

95 *Wooden figure, lacquered and painted in Temalacacingo, Guerrero. This is Mexico's national emblem. H approx. 9½" (24 cm).*

96, 97 *Lacquerwork with high-relief decoration, created with the technique of* rayado *in Olinalá, Guerrero.* TOP *Wooden tray. 15¾" x 11⅝" (40 x 29.5 cm).* ABOVE *Wooden dish by Josefa Ayala. D 7⅛" (18 cm).*

98, 99 *Lacquered wooden trays with encrusted designs, created with the technique of* embutido *in Uruapan, Michoacán.* TOP RIGHT *D 21¼" (54 cm).* ABOVE RIGHT *D 18½" (47 cm).*

100 OPPOSITE, ABOVE *Juniper wood inlaid with abalone shell from El Nith, Hidalgo. H of mirror 5¼" (13.2 cm). H of cross 2" (5.1 cm).*

101 OPPOSITE, BELOW *Lacquered wooden tray, from Uruapan, Michoacán. Encrusted designs show the dance of the Viejitos (Old Men). 12⅝" x 19½" (32 x 49.5 cm).*

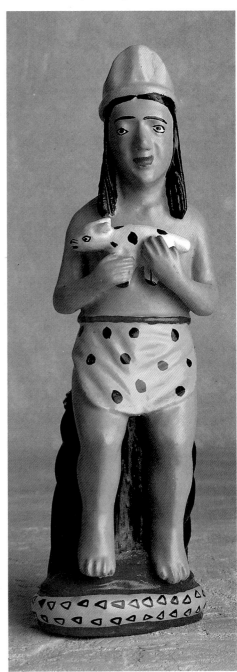

102 Wooden figure, carved and decorated with gloss paint by Fidel Navarro of Acapetlahuaya, Guerrero. It shows Cuauhtemoc, the last Aztec emperor, with a rabbit. At his feet is a coiled snake. H 10⅞" (27.7 cm).

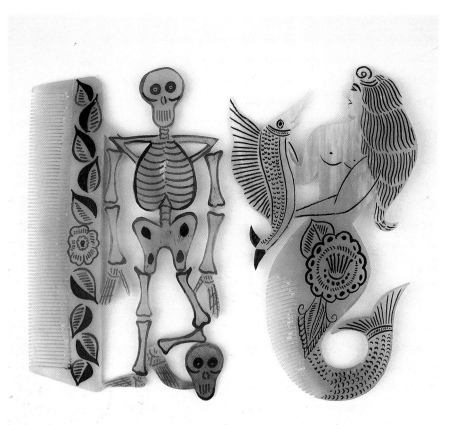

103 LEFT *Horn combs, with painted decoration, from San Antonio de la Isla, State of Mexico. (Left) Death 5¼" x 3¾" (13.2 x 9.5 cm). (Right) Mermaid 5¾" x 3⅛" (14.5 x 8 cm).*

104, 105 *Miniature figures of carved bone by Roberto Ruiz, Mexico City.* BELOW LEFT *The skeleton bride. H (excluding wooden base) 3" (7.7 cm).* BELOW RIGHT *The devil with skeletons. H (excluding wooden base) 2⅜" (6.1 cm).*

106 *Figures of painted tin made by Aarón Velasco Pacheco of Oaxaca city. D of sun 6" (15.2 cm).*

107 Heart of painted tin from Oaxaca city. H approx. 9⅞" (25 cm).

108, 109 Papier mâché creations by the Linares family of Mexico City. BELOW LEFT Brightly painted skulls with high-relief decoration. H approx. 15¾" (40 cm). BELOW RIGHT Articulated skeleton with glitter. H approx. 43¾" (111 cm).

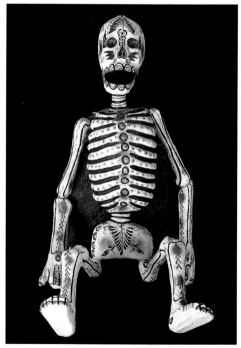

110 *Crow of wire and papier mâché, by Saulo Moreno. H 8⅝" (22 cm).*

TOYS AND MINIATURES

MEXICAN FOLK TOYS are among the most abundant and imaginative in the world. Fashioned from a vast range of materials, they reveal, possibly more than other crafts, the ingenuity and inventiveness of their creators. Yet because of the ephemeral nature and low selling price of their wares, toy-makers are rarely accorded the recognition their skills deserve. Toys are frequently overlooked for serious study, and Mexico has still to establish a museum for toys.

It is difficult to chart the early history of Mexican toys. Archaeological sites have yielded up numerous pottery artefacts that have the appearance of toys. According to most contemporary archaeologists, however, such items were probably funerary offerings or possessed some other ritual significance which placed them beyond the realm of children's playthings. While it seems hard to imagine that pre-Conquest parents developed no toys, it is known that babies were presented with miniature implements to prepare them symbolically for the tasks of adult life. Writing for the *Handbook of Middle American Indians*, William Madsen describes childhood among the modern Nahua:

> The Aztec pattern of teaching children to work when they are very young is still followed. In Ocotepec six-year-old girls help their mothers sweep, wash clothes, sew, and make *tortillas*. Eight-year-old boys help their fathers weed the fields, harvest the crops, tend the herds, care for the work animals, and carry home wood, charcoal and water.

In many country areas children make their own toys or play with whatever is available. Privileged children, whether they live in Mexico, Europe or the USA, can accumulate a profusion of toys during the course of a single year. But for children who live in isolated or impoverished regions, the acquisition of a new toy is a memorable event. A brightly painted whistle or a paper kite stimulates the imagination and offers an escape from the hard realities of life.

It is a paradox that although Mexican children begin being adults when they are practically children, adults never outgrow their childish delight in simple, amusing and beautiful things. Most toy-makers approach their work with genuine enjoyment and affection. Deploying wit and fantasy, they conjure up a make-believe world which can delight grown-ups as well as children. Some craftsmen and craftswomen devote themselves exclusively to the creation of toys; for others production is seasonal.

As in other craft fields, contemporary toy-makers combine indigenous materials and methods with those from distant lands: native components such as

111 LEFT *Painted pottery typewriter, made by Adrián Luis González of Metepec in the State of Mexico. W 4³⁄₈" (11 cm).*

clay, wood, palm or bone were joined after the Conquest by lead, wax and other substances; imported techniques such as glass-blowing and papier mâché were added to pre-Hispanic skills. This fusion led in the nineteenth century to a golden age for toys. The end of Spanish rule saw an influx of dolls, soldiers and other playthings from Europe, providing inspiration for Mexican craftworkers and enlarging the scope of nationally produced toys.

Today, various categories of toy exist. For the baby, enveloped in the folds of its mother's shawl, there are rattles made from gourds, papier mâché or interwoven palm leaves; these are filled with seeds or tiny pebbles. Potters continue as in pre-Hispanic times to fashion a quantity of figurines by hand and with the aid of moulds. Toys from the Mixtec community of Jamiltepec in Oaxaca are pre-Conquest in inspiration and style (pl. 113). In potting communities many children learn at a remarkably young age how to handle clay. In Amatenango del Valle, Chiapas, craft training can take precedence over formal education: until recently numerous children spent their days at home instead of attending the village school. A taste for commerce is acquired equally young: few visitors to Amatenango have the strength to resist when potters aged seven and eight relentlessly push forward their baskets. These are filled to overflowing with tiny

ABOVE LEFT *Mazahua child from San Simón de la Laguna in the State of Mexico.* ABOVE *Pre-Conquest pottery animal, possibly a jaguar, on wheels (AD 600–900). Excavated in the Huastec area of Pánuco, Veracruz, it is now in the Museo de Antropología in Xalapa. Legs and wheels were connected by wooden axles. Such creations may have the appearance of toys, but they probably possessed a ritual significance which placed them beyond the realm of children's playthings. Objects of this type prove that the principle of the wheel was understood in ancient Mexico, even if it was never used for transportation.*

Late Classic pottery figurine from Jaina which is also a whistle; the mouthpiece emerges from the head. This male Maya dignitary wears a profusion of ornaments and a head-dress with plumes and flowers.

but carefully modelled armadillos, peacocks, writhing snakes, elephants, dragons and other imaginary creatures (pl. 116).

In toy-making centres such as Santa Cruz de las Huertas, Jalisco, mould-made birds, animals and reptiles often have additional attributes. Lions, prancing horses or rotund, flower-sprigged pigs may prove to be money-banks. Clay whistles come in more guises still. In San Bartolo Coyotepec, Oaxaca, they take the form of glistening black mermaids playing guitars, cockerels, turkeys and fish on legs. Such is the modelling skill of these Zapotec potters that a visiting Australian cameraman was recently welcomed in one house with the gift of a specially made kangaroo whistle.

Musical toys are popular everywhere. Potters from San Bartolo Coyotepec make shiny black flutes, while striped clay trumpets from the State of Jalisco are often shaped with flaring jaws; clay bells in Aguasuelos, Veracruz, take the form of elegantly dressed women with wide skirts. Stringed instruments, introduced after the Conquest, have also entered the repertory of children's toys: wooden guitars from Paracho in Michoacán display exotic painted flowers.

During the nineteenth century dolls and puppets reached a high degree of sophistication. After a visit to Zacatecas in 1898 Frederick Starr, the North-American ethnographer, described the puppet company of Alejandro Aguirre for the British Folk-lore Society:

Aguirre makes his own puppets, and has some hundred and eighty figures representing different characters. The figures are jointed and made of wood. . . [they] range from fine ladies to dancing girls, from drunken news-vendors to priests, matadors, and officials. . . . They are made to walk, run, move their arms most naturally, dance, embrace, and engage in all sorts of pranks.

These achievements were slight when compared with those of Leandro Rosete Aranda. Based in Mexico City for much of the year, Aranda's famous company had a cast of more than five thousand puppets in 1900. Magnificently clothed by tailors and dressmakers, they performed against a succession of *trompe l'oeil* backdrops to the music of a live orchestra. The vogue for puppet theatres has long since passed; in Mexico City, however, puppets of a simpler type were made until recently by the late Manuel Ibarra Ramírez (pl. 117). His creations have little in common with the male puppets on strings that are now offered to tourists outside hotels: with their wide-brimmed straw hats and white cotton drawers, they conform to the stereotype foreign advertisers rely on to promote Mexican tequila or tortilla chips.

Nineteenth-century dolls, sometimes shown in paintings of the time, could be elegant creatures, but whereas imported dolls were often blessed with porcelain hands and faces, those made in Mexico had usually to rely on wax or painted wood. Today cloth-and-sawdust bodies are still fitted with finely moulded wax heads and limbs in the city of Puebla. With their gold-painted necklaces and luxuriant blonde or black tresses, they offer a reminder of times gone by. Old moulds are also responsible in the town of Celaya for dolls of papier mâché with articulated limbs (pl. 124). These glamorous beauties in bathing-suits, reminiscent of Hollywood starlets from the 1930s, proudly bear their names in glitter across their chests.

Country dolls are homelier by far: primitive wooden dolls are carved and painted with aniline colours in Ahuacatán, Guerrero; rag dolls with stocking faces are still to be found at rural fairs. In Chiapas Tzotzil women and small girls from San Juan Chamula fashion dolls from clay or cloth and dress them in miniature *huipiles* with wrap-around skirts (pl. 122); alternatively they use the dried husks of corncobs. These engaging figures have long corn-silk braids entwined with coloured yarn.

Some toy-makers rely exclusively on plant materials for their creations. Brilliantly dyed palm strands, for example, are skilfully deployed in the states of Mexico and Puebla. Production includes rainbow snakes with open jaws. These are known as '*tragadedos*' (finger-swallowers) or '*pescanovias*' (sweetheart-traps). The trick resides in getting an unsuspecting victim to insert his or her finger; when the snake is pulled the jaws tighten, painlessly holding the victim prisoner.

Movement is often achieved with ingeniously simple devices. Santa Cruz de las Huertas is the home of clay roundabouts which spin, and circus acrobats who balance precariously at the tops of poles. Colourfully lacquered Ferris wheels of gourds and wood carry diminutive passengers in Temalacacingo; delicately feathered fighting cocks from different towns wage battle, vibrating on their slender wires. This fascination with movement is especially apparent in the State of Guanajuato: tin butterflies on wheels flap their wings in Celaya, while from Santa Cruz de Juventino Rosas and Silao come jointed wooden snakes with red protruding tongues, weighted pink chickens that peck from acorn-cap dishes, and bizarre boxing matches between Death and the Devil which take place at the touch of a knob.

The modern age has revolutionized factory toys but it has also brought inspiration to the field of crafts. Helicopters and aeroplanes, perhaps only glimpsed in the torn pages of newspapers, are fashioned by the lacquer-workers of Temalacacingo, who paint windows full of passengers' faces on to the sides of toys (pl. 126). Purépecha women in Ocumicho, Michoacán, are also happy to interpret twentieth-century machines in clay; these often have devils and skeletons clinging to the wings of aeroplanes or clambering over the roofs of crowded buses. There is even a man outside the town of Xalapa, Veracruz, who

In this scene from Aztec daily life, a fourteen-year-old girl is taught to weave by her mother; over her head the scribe has drawn two large tortillas, her recommended daily ration. In modern Mexico Indian boys and girls are still taught craft skills at an early age.

builds ingenious trucks, with bottle-top wheels, from the stiff plastic mesh of shopping bags. Sometimes unusual toys are made by toy-makers for their own children. To amuse his small daughter, Adrián Luis González of Metepec, widely known for his splendid trees of life, has modelled a small typewriter of painted clay: perfect in every detail, it even has a plaque with the name Olivetti.

In his book *Juguetes Mexicanos*, Carlos Espejel has written with nostalgia about the seasonal nature of toys and games:

> During the course of a year there was a time for playing with one thing or another, but never two together. All these various toys interlocked to form a network which kept the infantile imagination busy throughout the year. For Mexican children the year was divided not into months but seasons: there was a time for kites, during the windy months of February and March, for spinning-tops, for yo-yos and for marbles . . . .

Mexican festivities continue, despite changing mores, to play an important role in the lives of many children and to extend the scope of toys and amusements. As Holy Week approaches, paper-workers in Mexico City and Celaya devote their skills to the elaboration of 'Judases'. These grotesque papier mâché figures, inspired originally by Judas Iscariot, take the form of grinning, red-painted devils, skeletons, *charros* and moustachioed dandies; alternatively they may caricature unpopular figures or portray popular ones such as Cantinflas, the Mexican comedian. Today Judases are rarely sold by street vendors, who even in the 1970s would display them grouped together on tall poles. They can still be admired in Mexico City, however, where they hang in colourful profusion outside the famous Sonora Market.

Traditionally Judases were decked out with fireworks and intended for public burning. On Easter Saturday, known in Mexico as the Saturday of Glory, they were brought out after Mass into village squares and city streets. To the jeers of the crowd these ill-fated figures would then disintegrate in a shower of stars and golden rain. According to Frederick Starr, Judases in 1898 were 'often filled with things for the rabble – meat, soap, bread, clothing, candy, etc. The people scramble for these, and run their chances of being hurt by the exploding *cuetes* [rockets]'. New laws that restrict the use of gunpowder, together with recent changes affecting the timing of the Mass, have virtually put an end to such celebrations in many parts of the country.

The feast of Corpus Christi in June has given rise to one of Mexico's most beautiful folk toys: *mulitas*, or mules. Made from palm, rushes, wheatstraw, banana wood or the dried husks of corn cobs, they may be small enough to pin on a lapel or large enough to carry a child. On this day during the Colonial era, when the inhabitants of Mexico came to pay their dues to the Church, they

Seller of papier mâché Judas figures, photographed outside La Merced market in Mexico City during the 1960s.

would often leave their mules tethered outside. The giving of *mulitas* is widely thought to commemorate this custom. In the atrium of the capital's cathedral, as in other parts of Mexico, toy mules are lined up for sale and their panniers filled with fruit and flowers.

September, marked by Independence celebrations, brings forth papier mâché helmets and trumpets. Painted red, green and white, they proclaim the colours of the Mexican flag. On 12 December, in honour of the Virgin of Guadalupe, *mestizo* children dressed in Indian styles visit provincial churches. Little girls wear colourful necklaces, shawls and embroidered blouses. Accompanying them are boys with *sarapes*, sandals and painted moustaches; they are called *Dieguitos* in memory of Juan Diego, the lowly Indian who saw the Virgin soon after the Conquest in a miraculous apparition. On their backs children carry small wooden frames hung with a multitude of tiny pots, gourds and other typically 'Indian' objects. Local and itinerant photographers, in competition with one another, offer specially constructed scenarios which resemble miniature film sets. In the capital similar scenes take place during Corpus Christi.

As Christmas draws near, markets everywhere begin to fill with figures for *nacimientos*, or nativity scenes. When Frederick Starr was in Mexico these were generally of wax. One *nacimiento*, which he described in detail, occupied the entire side of a room. It featured 'a landscape composed of rockwork and representing hills and valleys, a train of packmules and an attack of bandits'. The Garden of Eden formed the central piece. Next to it, however, was the Expulsion from Eden which showed Adam and Eve 'going forth into a scene of festivity – farms, cows being milked, crops being gathered, old women contentedly smoking, a band of musicians playing, and a company of young people gaily dancing'.

Contemporary *nacimiento* figures are usually made from clay in San Pedro Tlaquepaque, Jalisco (pl. 134). Many old moulds are still in use. Sometimes potters work all year for this one festival, even camping out with their wares from early November in distant towns and cities. Nativity scenes in many *mestizo* homes are no less spectacular than the one described above. Figures, which are acquired over many years, often come in a strange assortment of sizes: sheep may tower over elephants; the infant Jesus can dwarf the Three Kings.

Nativity scenes provide much amusement for children although their purpose is fundamentally serious. *Piñatas* are devised solely for children, however. Made to be broken, these exotic creations are nevertheless fashioned with enormous care. Ships, stars, flowers and animals are constructed from papier mâché and covered with tissue paper of different colours; more recent additions range from Donald Duck to Batman. Inside each *piñata* is a clay pot (illus. p. 71). These pots are packed to the brim by purchasers with candies, fruit, nuts and small toys. The *piñata* is then suspended high in the air. One by one children are blind-

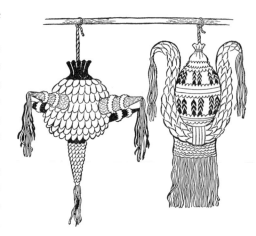

Christmas piñatas *in traditional shapes; although the exterior is made of paper, a sturdy clay pot within contains fruit and candies (illus. p. 71).*

The theme of death inspires many toys. Makers share the black humour inherent in the engravings of José Guadalupe Posada. Working at the turn of the century, this gifted artist used skulls and skeletons to show the transitory nature of earthly pursuits, and to ridicule leading figures of the time. This engraving, which shows a fashionable lady in the guise of a skeleton, is known as la calvera catrina.

folded, spun round, and given a stick with which to hit out at the tantalizing treasure-trove above. The excitement builds until a sudden crash is heard: broken at last, the pot pours out its contents over the crowd beneath (pl. 88).

In a few places the Christmas season is still characterized by *posadas*. These are parties which take place on the nine successive nights leading up to Christmas: participants gather to re-enact the biblical journey made by Joseph and Mary from Nazareth to Bethlehem. By tradition, presents are not given to children until 6 January, feast of the Santos Reyes (Holy Kings). Contact with the USA, together with sales drives by advertisers and city stores, are affecting Mexican customs, however. The Three Kings are being gradually supplanted by Father Christmas, while *nacimientos* in many homes are giving way to Christmas trees laden with artificial snow.

Despite the pervasive effects of Halloween on Day of the Dead celebrations, a peculiarly Mexican attitude to death is still expressed by toy-makers in an astonishing variety of ways. In the words of one toy-maker, 'Our children grow up with death. When they are small they play with death. For us it is another part of life. . . . ' With the approach of November, markets and craft shops begin to fill with toy coffins, cardboard skeletons that dance at the pull of a string, and clay skulls with movable lower jaws. From the town of Guanajuato come coffin-bearing priests, with chick-pea heads, on a moving belt: when a handle is turned, the funeral procession glides swiftly into the gaping jaws of Hell.

Strangest and perhaps most fantastic of all are the tiny clay skeletons which are made in Oaxaca city and other places. Portrayed in the midst of everyday activities, they recall the nineteenth-century engravings of Manuel Manilla and José Guadalupe Posada. These grimly humorous figures include wedding couples, footballers, priests hearing confession, policemen, and even skeletons praying on their knees at the graveside of dead relatives.

Many of these toys are extremely small. Pre-Conquest sites such as Tzintzuntzan in Michoacán have yielded up a quantity of diminutive jars and dishes. Like the miniature garments that have been found in dry caves in the State of Oaxaca, they probably served as votive offerings; even today, in the Nahua village of Atla in Puebla, a few women still create tiny garments which they leave on a neighbouring hillside. The current popularity of miniatures in Mexico may partially derive, therefore, from their ritual importance within ancient cultures.

Tiny baskets, brooms, cauldrons, grinding stones, jugs and plates are patiently fashioned by craftworkers everywhere. The inhabitants of Puebla State offer an unusually wide range of miniatures. Pink rabbits just a few millimetres high, patchwork lizards and pigs with curly tails are made from strips of dyed palm in Santa María Chigmecatitlán. Enticing glass dishes full of rainbow fruits, and tempting chicken dinners sprinkled with sesame seeds turn the shelves of display cabinets into delectable restaurants. Even more skilfully contrived, however, are kitchen tableaux, complete with old-style ranges: the walls are hung from floor to ceiling with cooking pots, while in the foreground plump and smiling cooks of painted clay chop food on wooden tabletops. Some of these minuscule scenes are set in glass-fronted wooden boxes but others, smaller still, fit snugly inside a walnut shell.

Some materials are particularly suited to the creation of miniatures. Glass centres in the cities of Puebla and Mexico are virtual Noah's Arks. With the heat of the gas-jet, sticks of glass are transformed into alligators, fighting cocks and antlered stags. A few miniaturists are acknowledged masters in their field. The work of Roberto Ruiz has been described in Chapter V. Nazario Trujillo retains a skill that has become extremely rare: he dresses fleas. Dead insects are not only costumed but grouped into elaborate scenes such as weddings.

Until the nineteenth century the word 'toys' applied in England not just to the playthings of children, but also to a variety of small objects which were initially of slight value. In modern Mexico miniatures are frequently collected by adults and displayed in cabinets; many toys are similarly situated on the borderline between ornament and plaything. Writers, painters and photographers have long admired even the most basic of children's toys for their imaginative force and vitality. Visitors to Frida Kahlo's house, which she occupied with Diego Rivera from 1929 to 1954, can still see the immense Judas figures that guarded the entrance, and examine the dolls, clay roundabouts and skeletons that gave her such pleasure. Mexican toys still embody many of the qualities that the Surrealist André Breton most admired in Mexico. Theirs is a world where the irrational and the unexpected abound.

Sadly the qualities that attract many adults now alienate growing numbers of children. In towns and cities, cinema and television, modern sports facilities and the constant presence of the machine age have robbed many hand-made toys of their excitement and power to entertain. Diminutive clay cooking pots, pecking chickens and palm-leaf lizards may correspond to daily life in rural areas, but hold little magic for urban children who grow up among cars. Clay whistles in the shape of three-headed monsters may feed the imagination of village children, but fail to satisfy their counterparts in cities who follow the adventures of Batman and know about space travel.

The insecure future of hand-made toys is further jeopardized by economic hardship. Despite the meticulous work which goes into many toys, prices are often pitifully low. Large numbers of traditional toys are made today by elderly craftworkers, and it seems unlikely that their descendants will willingly continue production for the same narrow margin of profit. Meanwhile the output of factory-made toys is steadily rising, competing with folk toys even in remote country markets. However sad the reality, it seems unlikely that many of the toys and miniatures described will still be with us in the twenty-first century.

112 RIGHT *Painted pottery piggy-bank, made from an old mould by Tiburcio Soteno of Metepec, State of Mexico. H 9⅝" (24.5 cm).*

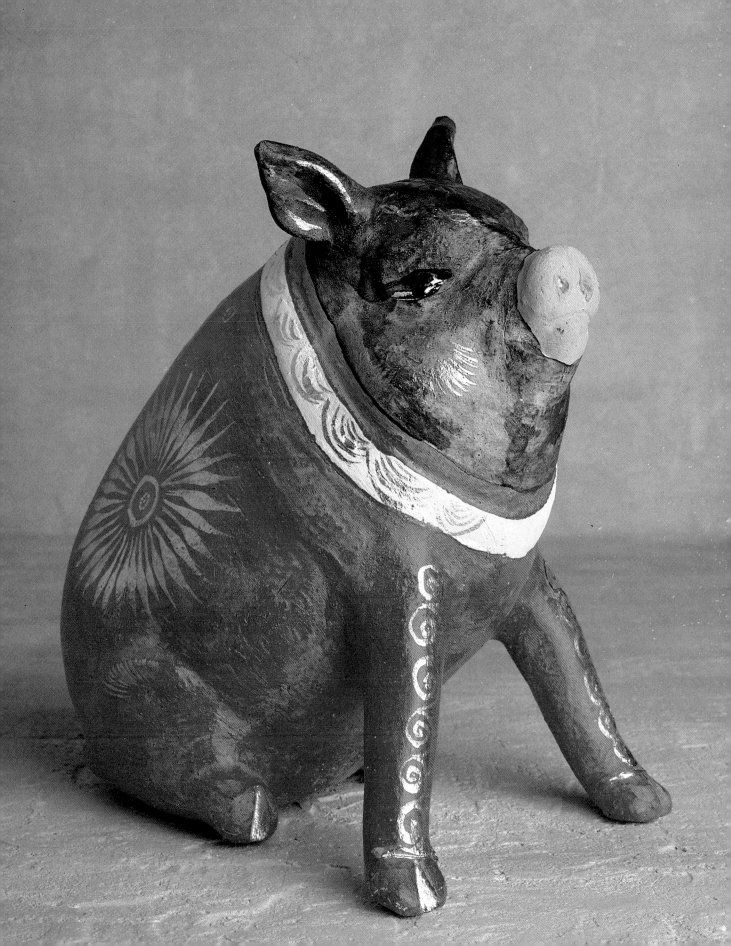

113 BELOW LEFT *Painted pottery figures from the Mixtec community of Jamiltepec, Oaxaca. H of women 4¾" (12 cm).*

114 BELOW *Pottery money-bank in the shape of a cat, painted with earth colours, from the Nahua village of San Augustín de las Flores, Guerrero. H 7¼" (18.5 cm).*

115 *Pottery whistle in the shape of a rabbit, decorated with industrial colours, from the Purépecha village of Ocumicho, Michoacán. H 6⅛" (15.5 cm).*

116 *Pottery animals from Amatenango del Valle, Chiapas. Modelled by Tzeltal children, they are painted with earth colours. Average H 1⅝" (4 cm).*

117 *Puppets with clay heads, arms and feet attached to cloth, made in Mexico City by Manuel Ibarra Ramírez. H (without feathers) approx. 6⅛″ (15.5 cm).*

118 *Cloth mermaids with wool hair from the State of Oaxaca. H 9" (23 cm).*

119 BELOW LEFT *Cloth dolls with woollen pigtails, in Mazahua costume, by Enriqueta Bernardino Gómez in the village of San Felipe Santiago, State of Mexico. H 11" (28 cm).*

120 BELOW *Cloth dolls in Tehuana costume with ribbons in their hair, from the State of Oaxaca. H 8½" (21.5 cm).*

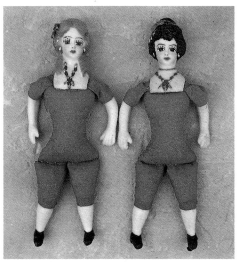

121 ABOVE *Dolls with cloth bodies from Puebla city. Heads and limbs are of wax. H 7½" (19 cm).*

122 LEFT *Three rag dolls. (Left) stocking face and hair, from Jalisco. H 6¾″ (17 cm). (Centre) Tzotzil doll in village costume with woollen braids, from San Juan Chamula, Chiapas. H 5⅛″ (13 cm). (Right) Tzotzil mother and baby in village costume; her braids are of corn silk. From San Juan Chamula, Chiapas. H 7¼″ (18.5 cm).*

123 BELOW *Wax dolls. Dressed in Tzotzil costume from the village of Zinacantán, they were made in the town of San Cristóbal de las Casas, Chiapas. H 5⅞″ (15 cm).*

124 RIGHT *Articulated papier mâché dolls, decorated with paint and glitter, from the town of Celaya, Guanajuato. H of centre doll 16¾″ (42.5 cm).*

125 Wooden creatures which move on sticks.
H of horse 4⅞" (12.5 cm).

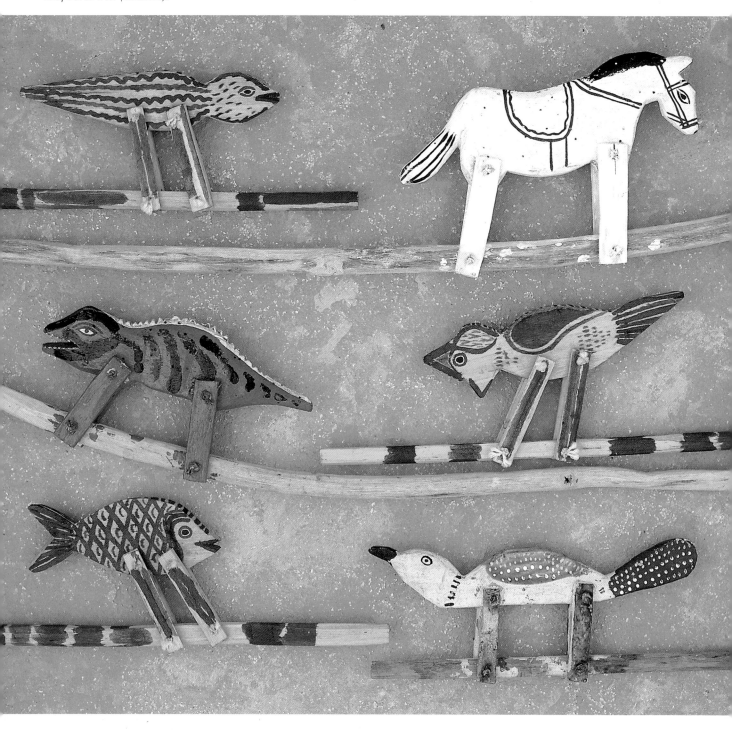

126 LEFT *Lacquered wooden helicopter, with painted passengers, from Temalacacingo, Guerrero. H 3⅞" (10 cm).*

127 ABOVE *Mould-made skeleton acrobat of painted pottery from Santa Cruz de las Huertas, Jalisco. H approx. 4¾" (12 cm).*

128 BELOW *Wooden car from Pátzcuaro, Michoacán. L 6¼" (15.7 cm).*

129 RIGHT *Lacquered roundabout, with painted decoration, of gourds and wood; Temalacacingo, Guerrero. H 11" (28 cm).*

130 *Papier mâché masks from Celaya,*
Guanajuato. Average H 9" (23 cm).

131 LEFT *Wooden tiger with sequin eyes from the region of Pahuatlán, Puebla. H 5⅛" (13 cm).*

132 ABOVE *Wooden lizards and iguanas, lacquered and painted in Temalacacingo, Guerrero. Average L 6¼" (16 cm).*

133 RIGHT *Plastic wrestlers from Mexico City. Although toys of this type are mould-made, they are finished off by hand. Average H 4⅜" (11 cm).*

134 *Pottery devil and two coiled snakes,*
decorated with industrial gloss paint. Such
figures are made in San Pedro Tlaquepaque,
Jalisco, for nativity scenes. H of devil 4⅞" (12.5 cm).

135 *Skeleton doll with floral dress, made from*
wire and clay in the State of Oaxaca. H 7⅞"
(20 cm).

136 BELOW *Brightly painted articulated paper skeletons from the State of Mexico; when strings are pulled the limbs move. Such toys are made for the Festival of the Dead. H of tallest figure 16⅞" (43 cm).*

137, 138 *Painted wooden toys from the city of Oaxaca.* ABOVE RIGHT *When the handle at the side is turned, the skeletons move their limbs. H 17½" (44.5 cm).* RIGHT *Wooden roundabout. H 20⅞" (53 cm).*

139 LEFT, MAIN PICTURE *Miniature skeleton widow of painted clay, with glittering black lace on her cotton-wool hair. H 4⅞″ (12.5 cm).*

140, 141 *Miniature figures of painted pottery skeletons, made for the Festival of the Dead.* INSET LEFT, TOP *Wedding couple. H 2⅞″ (7.5 cm).* INSET LEFT, BOTTOM *Market seller with diminutive palm fans. H approx. 2¼″ (5.5 cm).*

142 *Miniature tiger masks of wood with real teeth and whiskers, from the State of Guerrero. H of largest 3½″ (9 cm).*

CHAPTER VII

CEREMONIAL AND EPHEMERAL ARTS

IN THE PRE-HISPANIC WORLD, religion permeated every aspect of life. This is still true in Indian Mexico today, particularly among the Huichol of the western Sierra Madre. Isolated by high mountain ranges, members of this marginal group continue to worship a pantheon of deities associated with the forces of nature. Looked on with awe, but also with affection, they are known by terms of close kinship.

Grandfather Fire is the special protector of the Huichol. In the earliest times he taught them how to please the other gods, and he continues to watch over his followers today. Fire provides warmth and cooks their food; it also lights up the darkness and clears the land for planting. Nakawé, or Grandmother Growth, is another important netherworld deity. She is the source of spring water and vegetation. It is to her that requests for a good harvest, long life and the health of children are most often made. Included among the deities of the upper realm is Father Sun. Born in ancient times to light and warm the earth by day, this ambivalent god can also send illness and drought.

Prolonged efforts by Franciscan missionaries have led the Huichol to adopt some Catholic feast days and ritual elements. In general, however, Christianity has had little impact on Huichol belief. Carl Lumholtz, who documented the customs of this proud people at the end of the last century, recorded a telling comment by one of his informants: 'If Christians pray to the saints that are made by carpenters, why should not the Huichol pray to the sun which is so much better made?'

The Huichol have their own mythological view of history, which is passed down orally from generation to generation and guarded by shamans, or *mará'akáte*. Huichol folklore is by no means static; as new things are absorbed from the outside world, myths evolve to explain them from a Huichol perspective. *Mará'akáte* need excellent memories: one anthropologist noted that a shaman of his acquaintance could sing the equivalent of over four hundred manuscript pages of myths. Physical endurance is another requisite: sometimes *mará'akáte* must chant for days and nights on end, accompanying themselves on the violin. Children learn about their heritage by listening; for most this is the only formal education they will receive.

Collective belief finds expression in festivals and pilgrimages. Dependent for their survival on maize, the Huichol hold numerous ceremonies to honour the various stages of its growth. Other agricultural events include the Feast of the Ripe Fruits, when the faithful thank the gods for the new harvest. The year-long

143 LEFT *Lacquered wooden mask decorated with ribbons for the dance of* Los Negros, *from Michoacán. The animal hide hangs down the dancer's back. H of mask 7½" (19 cm).*

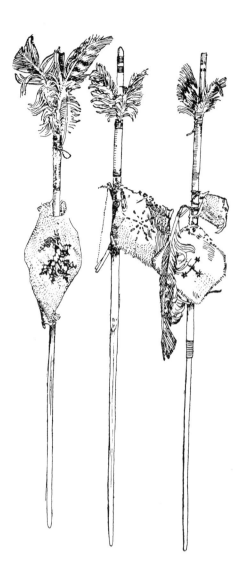

cycle of festivities would not be complete, however, without the many rituals connected with *peyote* – the hallucinatory cactus that inspires the Huichol throughout their lives. The cult of this small grey-green plant, known to botanists as *Lophorora Williamsii*, has a long history in Mexico. After the Conquest the Spaniards tried to abolish its use wherever possible, believing it to be the instrument of the devil, but a few groups in remote surroundings escaped their jurisdiction.

Peyote in Huichol society has the status of a god. According to mythology, he first appeared on earth as a giant deer, causing small plants to spring up wherever he trod. When Huichol hunters followed with their bows and arrows, the deer disappeared, and in its place they found a large *peyote* growing. Today *peyote* is still identified with the deer, who is also divine and the hero of numerous legends. Capable of many metamorphoses, this magical animal is similarly viewed as an incarnation of maize. Together the three forces form a trinity, where each is an incarnation of the other.

Wirikúta, the land where the sacred cacti grow, lies far outside Huichol territory in the high desert of San Luis Potosí. Once a year small bands of pilgrims leave their homes to gather *peyote*. This arduous quest is akin to a hunting ritual, for the tiny plants are shot with bows and arrows as if they were deer. The chief *peyote* festival takes place after the return of pilgrims. With music, songs and dance they retrace their search for the sacred cactus. Those who take it admit it is tough and extremely bitter, but say they are rewarded by the brilliantly coloured visions, the heightened perception and the sense of euphoria which are induced by the plant's high mescaline content. Among the Huichol, *peyote* is seen as a divine gift which puts them in touch with the gods.

In order to win the protection and goodwill of these many deities, the Huichol also express their faith in individual ways. Private pilgrimages to sacred caves, rocks and springs are regularly undertaken. Food and votive objects are presented during even the simplest of ceremonies. Highly creative as a people, the Huichol dedicate unlimited time and skill to the preparation of elaborate offerings which will give a concrete form to their desires. Open-air altars display a profusion of gifts during festivals; throughout the year sacred images are kept in circular temples and ritual objects are left at natural shrines.

Chief among these offerings are votive arrows, for they carry the requests of the maker straight to the gods. Miniature objects tied to the shaft symbolize special demands. Stuck upright in the ground during ceremonies, the arrows are then thought of as 'sacrificed', and supplicants know that their prayers have been heard. *Tsikuri*, or 'gods' eyes', are made from strands of brightly coloured yarn; these are stretched on to bamboo crosses to form lozenges through which deities can watch their followers. Worn by children during the Feast of the Ripe Fruits, they serve as requests for health and long life.

Huichol prayer-arrows with tiny examples of embroidery. Before embarking on textile work, many women make votive offerings to ask the gods for help and goodwill. This illustration and the one on page 30 were drawn by Carl Lumholtz nearly ninety years ago.

Votive bowls are a favourite gift. It is hoped that when the gods come to use them, they will 'drink in' the prayers of the faithful and grant what is asked. Bowls are made by coating the inside of half-gourds with wax, and forming decorative designs with seeds, maize kernels, minute pebbles, and coins. Sometimes wads of cotton wool are added to symbolize the white fleecy clouds that bring rain and life to the Huichol.

Since their introduction glass beads have proved popular, and today many gourds are entirely lined with them. Picked up one by one on the point of a needle or thorn, the tiny beads are dextrously pressed down into the wax to form brightly coloured pictures featuring suns, birds, animals, butterflies and flowers. Sometimes designs convey the hopes of the maker – a deer shaped by a hunter might be a plea for divine help on a future hunting expedition. Alternatively gourds may display scenes from mythology or ceremonial life. *Peyote* pilgrims are shown on their way to Wírikúta (pl. 148), while other designs recall the deluge from Huichol mythology (pl. 147). One day, so it is told, a Huichol man was clearing his fields for planting when Grandmother Growth warned him of an approaching flood; she advised him to make a boat and to carry with him five grains of maize, five beans and a black bitch. All this he did. After five years the waters subsided, and the goddess caused the vegetation and the wildlife to reappear. The dog became a woman; with her the man had a large family, and their descendants re-peopled the earth.

Religious devotion finds another outlet in the *nierika*, or 'countenance'. Fashioned from stone, from reeds interwoven with thread, or from small wooden boards covered with wax and yarn, these round and square offerings depict the 'face' of things and supernatural forces. The last few decades have seen the emergence of the 'yarn painting', suggested by the *nierika*. Wax, softened by the sun's heat, is spread evenly over a wooden board. Using a sharp instrument, the artist then scratches on the design and lays down the outlines with strands of wool or acrylic. Spaces are filled in as yarns are pressed firmly down into the wax. Reminiscent of *peyote* visions, yarn paintings combine vibrant colours with complex symbols. One example (pl. 145) includes a stylized representation of the sacred cactus, *peyote*, and a maize plant; the shaman is apparently performing a ceremony in their honour. Pictures, like some beaded bowls, are now made for commercial ends. Bought by galleries and collectors, they provide makers with a welcome source of income, yet they continue to reflect Huichol beliefs and to draw inspiration from mythology and ritual.

For the Huichol life is precarious. Throughout much of the year they face hunger and malnutrition, yet material privations are looked on with indifference. Despite their poverty the Huichol feel rich in their *kupuri*, roughly translatable as 'soul', and they are sustained by an unshakeable faith in the meaningfulness of all things. Change may affect other areas of Mexico, but it seems certain that the next generation will adhere to these ancient beliefs. Future shamans will continue to serve the gods and to chant the sacred songs of the Huichol race, like this one in honour of Wírikúta:

What beautiful hills, what beautiful hills,
so green here where we are.
Do not weep, brothers, do not weep,
we have come here to be happy,
we have taken this path
to find our lives.

For we are all,
we are all the children
of a flower of brilliant colours,
of a burning flower.
And here there is no one
who regrets what we are . . .

In the Otomí village of San Pablito, Puebla, seed spirits are used in rituals to promote growth and to encourage crop yields. Cut from bark paper, they are shown with mature fruits or vegetables protruding from their sides.
ABOVE *The Spirit of the Tomato.*
OPPOSITE *The Spirit of the Banana.*

Although most other Indian groups have adopted Catholicism, pre-Conquest beliefs and practices have been simultaneously retained in many villages. This is so in San Pablito, Puebla, where Otomí villagers attribute all things, whether good or bad, to spirit beings associated with the sky, the earth, the underworld and water. Bark-paper cut-outs, representing the life-force of these spirits, are used in curing and fertility ceremonies. Shamans are powerful figures: their links with the spirit world enable them to win goodwill from benevolent forces and to ward off malign ones. Christianity is not perceived as antithetical to these beliefs. It provides villagers with a parallel series of rituals while the priest, who occasionally visits San Pablito, is seen as a ritual specialist operating in a different sphere. Sometimes Catholic saints have even fused with Otomí spirits.

In their book *Traditional Papermaking and Paper Cult Figures of Mexico*, Alan R. Sandstrom and Pamela Effrein Sandstrom have analysed the roles played by these supernatural forces. In San Pablito images, made from single sheets of bark paper or from several layers of tissue paper, are brought to life in various ways. The shaman can breathe into their mouths, hold them in incense smoke, or sprinkle them with alcohol. The Queen of the Bad Earth, the President of Hell and the Lords of Lightning, Thunder and the Rainbow belong to the Underworld. Earth forces include the Earth Mother, the Lord of the Mountain and a vast number of seed spirits. Shown with mature fruits or vegetables protruding from their sides, seed spirits are used in rituals to encourage crop yields.

Many people in San Pablito now augment their income by offering embroideries and beadwork to outsiders (pls 35, 36, 39). The manufacture and

sale of bark paper has been described in Chapter V. Cut-out figures have also found a market with collectors and tourists; the Spirit of the Pineapple, for example, is shown surrounded by beans, birds and deer (pl. 85). Pictures and replica figures have great decorative value, yet it should not be forgotten that they portray a highly complex and extremely ancient view of the world. The spirit pantheon of San Pablito represents a constant danger to the community; only through public and private rituals may divine protection be won and harm averted.

Curing ceremonies, which free the patient from evil forces, are commonplace in many parts of Mexico. Healers generally rely on incense and on a range of medicinal plants, but a few still use pottery figures which could be mistaken by the uninitiated for toys. In Tlayacapan, Morelos, brightly painted clay is shaped to resemble animals, people and a bedridden patient; when the ritual is over and the figures are deemed to have absorbed the patient's sickness, they are abandoned on the hillside. Similar figures, made in Metepec by the late Modesta Fernández, were used until recently in the State of Mexico.

Before the Conquest the gods stimulated artistic endeavour at every level; every home had an altar and every act was accomplished through the favour of some deity. Today it is the Catholic religion that serves as a catalyst for creativity throughout most of Mexico. House altars and churches are a focus for devotion to the Virgin Mary and the Saints; their images are carved in wood by *santeros*, or saint-carvers, who are highly respected for their skills. Sometimes, as described in Chapter II, the saints are dressed in Indian clothing and adorned in accordance with local styles.

Milagros, mentioned in Chapter III, remain an important element of Catholic worship; throughout Mexico the robes of popular saints are often entirely covered with tiny arms, legs and hearts (pl. 56). *Retablos*, painted on tin or paper, give thanks in pictorial form for divine intervention; illness and accidents are depicted in detail and accompanied by words to describe the miracle. In remote areas where there is no resident priest, villagers have charge of local churches and are largely responsible for their decoration. The lacquer-workers of Olinalá, Guerrero, have made their church one of the most beautiful in all Mexico. Walls and altar are panelled with a mass of gleaming lacquer, and the lampshades have been replaced by richly decorated gourds that hang suspended from the ceiling.

Festivities of the Conquest period were described in vivid terms by Spanish chroniclers. In rural areas, where life is often extremely hard, festivals still mark the high point of village life. *Fiestas* commemorate Catholic holidays such as Christmas and honour the patron saint of a village or town. Sometimes outsiders express surprise at the high costs involved. Pleasurable as they may be, however, *fiestas* are undertaken for the most serious of reasons: participants believe they

Male dancer from Panotla, Tlaxcala, elegantly dressed for La Cuadrilla de Catrines *(literally, The Dandies' Quadrille) during* Carnaval. *Wooden masks, which are made in San Pablo Apetatitlán, are among the finest in Mexico. Once decorated with oil paints, they are rubbed with the crop of a dead chicken; this creates a protective and shiny coating. Masks have glass eyes, which open and shut when a thread is pulled.*

are ensuring the well-being of their families, and promoting divine harmony for the community at large.

Extensive preparations precede even the simplest of ceremonies. In potting villages special candlesticks and incense burners are made; cloths for wrapping food are woven or embroidered; ribbons, incense and other necessary articles may be bought in markets and fairs. In some regions huge wax candles, with the delicacy of lace or filigree, are displayed in churches and carried behind the saints during processions. Firework-makers in Puebla and other states construct immense bamboo towers, called *castillos* (castles). When darkness descends the lit fuse travels slowly upwards from storey to storey: rockets and catherine wheels ignite, bursting like flowers and stars, and filling the sky with cascades of light and colour.

Commercially made paper, like wax and gunpowder, was a Spanish importation. Today sheets of tissue and metallic paper are exquisitely perforated in the town of San Salvador Huixcolotla, Puebla. Artists such as Luis Vivanco and Maurilio Rojas work with several sheets at once; using a selection of sharp chisels to cut the paper, they hammer out figurative designs for every occasion (pl. 160). Often brightly coloured, these lacy papercuts are suspended on threads outside town and village churches. Some Totonac near Papantla, Veracruz, also prepare papercuts for ceremonial events; using scissors and razor blades they pattern tissue paper with geometric designs, birds and vegetation.

In Indian Mexico offerings of food are taken to churches as they were once taken to pre-Hispanic temples. Wheat-flour bread, introduced from Europe, is shaped in a variety of ways. Purépecha women in Ocumicho, Michoacán, bake immense loaves which they decorate with bananas and pomegranates; they also dance, carrying bread figures in the form of horses, garlands of flowers and women wearing necklaces.

Throughout Mexico an infinity of other perishable materials are worked with skill and ingenuity. Beautiful and ephemeral archways of flowers and leaves are built round church doorways; paths of flower petals and dyed sawdust lead through the village of Patamban during the Feast of Cristo Rey; seed mosaics showing biblical scenes are carried by oxen in Metepec in honour of *San Isidro Labrador* (Saint Isidro the Farmer). In the city of Oaxaca, on 23 December, elongated radishes are carved and combined to depict dances, religious tableaux and the archaeological ruins of Mitla; doves and images of the Virgin Mary are also displayed, made from everlasting flowers and wire by the inhabitants of San Antonino. The Mazahua, many of whom live in villages not far from Mexico City, now rely on some surprising elements: churches may be embellished with swirls of popcorn, and saints festooned with garlands of flowers and Marie biscuits (illus. p. 8).

Many festivals are still dominated by dances, which vary according to region. Since the Conquest the fusion of Spanish and native traditions has created a range of dances and masks that few countries can equal. Performers are motivated by religious devotion; this may take the form of a *manda*, or vow, with dancers promising God and the saints that they will perform for a given number of years. Although wood is the material most often used for masks, they are also made from leather, clay, paper, cloth, wire mesh, gourds and wax. One of the most widespread dance-cycles in Mexico centres on the tiger (pls 9, 142). Of ancient origin, such dances probably featured jaguars or ocelots, because the tiger is not native to Mexico. 'Tiger' dances reflect the agricultural preoccupations of farming communities; in most versions the tiger damages the crops and is chased by angry farmers, who finally succeed in catching and killing their striped enemy. Other dances feature bulls, deer, goats, birds and a host of other creatures from the animal world.

Europeans, with their fair skins, facial hair and blue or green eyes, were a source of surprise and fascination for Mexican Indians. They also became a source of inspiration for mask-makers (pl. 154). Two important dance-cycles –

'Moors and Christians' and 'The Conquest' – show Spanish soldiers defending their homeland against Moorish invasion, and gaining victory over the peoples of ancient Mexico (pl. 153). *Conquistadores* from this last cycle are often led by *Santiago* (Saint James), who wears a wooden horse tied round his waist (pl. 156). Black settlers, brought to Mexico as slaves, also appear in several dances. According to Janet Brody Esser, black men are thought by the Purépecha of Michoacán to represent lords or principal beings who control the air (pl. 143). At the time of the Conquest many European dances had allegorical themes portraying the triumph of virtue and the downfall of evil. The devil, death, angels and the Deadly Sins still do battle at *fiesta* time in countless village squares in modern Mexico (pl. 155).

For many Mexicans the most important festival is that of the Dead. As the end of October approaches, Indians and *mestizos* alike prepare to receive the deceased, who have celestial permission to visit friends and relatives on earth. Celebrations, which can be extremely costly, vary from region to region, as does the timing of events. In Puebla State, 28 October belongs to *los accidentados*, or those who die in accidents. Dead children are welcomed on the 31st at midday. All Saints Day (1 November) sees their departure, and the arrival of the souls of adults. They will withdraw at midday on All Souls' Day, held since the late thirteenth century on 2 November.

All over Mexico tombs are tidied and embellished in honour of the returning dead. The windows of bread-shops are painted with cavorting skeletons and skulls. In the portals of Toluca and other cities, skulls of coloured sugar and marzipan figures are bought as gifts for the living and the dead (pls 157–59). House altars feature a profusion of flowers, leaves, fruits and bread figures; elaborately fashioned candlesticks and incense burners are set out with dishes of food. Care is taken to ensure that the aroma is strong, for it is the aroma or essence that the dead extract. Offerings for children are often served in diminutive vessels; adults may be given cigarettes and tequila. In parts of Michoacán villagers also hold all-night vigils in the graveyard, decorating tombs with portable cane altars hung with flowers and fruit. More usually, however, Mexicans gather in the graveyard on the morning of the 2nd. Sometimes the dead are serenaded by brass bands and *mariachi* musicians. To an outsider such celebrations might seem surprising, but in Mexico death is seen as a part of life. The dead are never forgotten, because once a year they return to take their place beside the living.

As the twentieth century draws to a close, the pace of change increases. In many villages nylon dresses and plastic bowls are replacing hand-woven *huipiles* and clay pots, yet the *fiesta* lives on. Vast sums of money, days of hard work and unstinting devotion are expended in the creation of beauty which will last just a few hours.

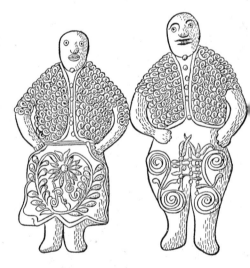

Panes de muertos, or the Bread of the Dead. Figures come in animal and human forms. Made in large city bakeries and in tiny hamlets, they are offered to the dead and enjoyed by the living.

144 *Huichol yarn picture from the State of Jalisco. Acrylic yarns have been pressed on to a wax-covered board. 23⅝" sq. (60 cm sq.).*

145, 146 *Huichol yarn pictures from the State of Jalisco.* TOP *Shaman with drum and religious paraphernalia. 31½″ sq. (80 cm sq.).* BOTTOM *Figures with temple; sacred objects include a god's eye and a prayer arrow. 23⅝″ sq. (60 cm sq.).*

147–50 *Votive gourds lined with wax; glass beads have been pressed down one by one on the point of a needle.* TOP LEFT *Flood, as described in Huichol mythology. D 8¼" (21 cm).* TOP RIGHT *Peyote pilgrims. D 7⅝" (19.5 cm).* BOTTOM LEFT *Deer and flowers. D 7½" (19 cm).* BOTTOM RIGHT *Deer and eagles. D 9⅞" (25 cm).*

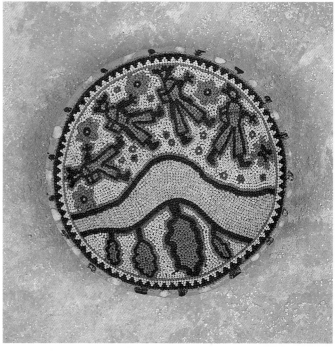

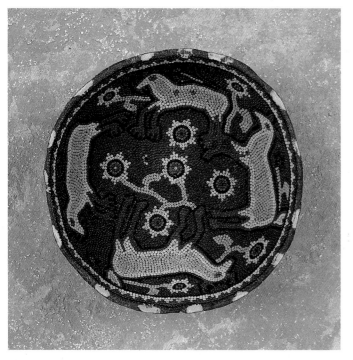

151, 152 Wooden masks, carved and painted with industrial gloss paints by Fidel Navarro, who also provides fellow-villagers in Acapetlahuaya, Guerrero, with figures of saints. Both masks are decorative. LEFT *The Devil*, with real horns and teeth. H (including horns) 20" (51 cm). BELOW *Christ*, with a movable jaw; the thorns are painted cocktail sticks. H 11½" (29 cm).

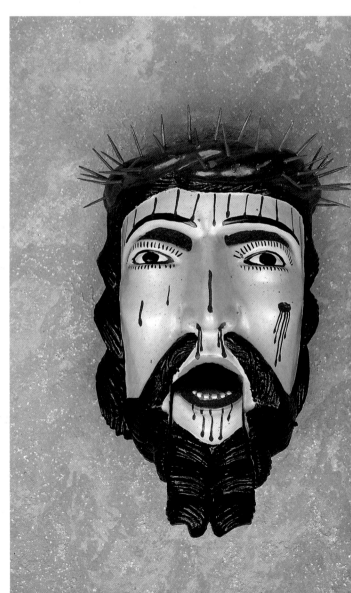

153 *Wooden mask in the likeness of a plumed Aztec warrior. State of Guerrero. H 13¾"* (35 cm).

154 *Four masks inspired by European physiognomy. Those in the top row are from the State of Guerrero. Those in the bottom row are from Chiapas (left) and Tlaxcala (right); both masks have glass eyes. H of mask lower left 6⅜" (16.2 cm).*

155 *Devil mask worn during celebrations in Teloloapan, Guerrero. Carved and painted with industrial gloss paints by Fidel de la Puente, it features writhing serpents. Real horns and sheep's wool have been used; the animal hide hangs down the wearer's back. H approx. 23⅝" (60 cm).*

156 *Carved wooden horses, painted with industrial gloss paint and embellished with horsehair manes by Fidel Navarro of Acapetlahuaya, Guerrero. Such horses are worn round the waist by dancers who take the role of* Santiago *(Saint James). H of larger horse approx. 9⅜" (24 cm).*

157–59 *Ephemeral creations for the Festival of the Dead, from the region of Toluca, State of Mexico.* RIGHT *Sugar figures filled with aniseed liquid: a guitar and a soul in purgatory. H of guitar 3⅛" (8 cm).* BELOW *Marzipan leaf with hand holding bouquet of roses. L 9¼" (23.5 cm).* BELOW RIGHT *Icing-sugar cat with paper adornments. H 5¾" (14.5 cm).*

160 *Papercut on a coloured background for the Festival of the Dead, by Maurilio Rojas of San Salvador Huixcolotla, Puebla. 20¼" x 29⅞" (51.5 x 76 cm).*

COLLECTING MEXICAN FOLK ART

In Mexico, as in other countries, it is usually more rewarding to travel with a purpose: in Mexico the pursuit of beautiful and striking objects can lead to an understanding of the cultures from which they spring, and can foster lasting friendships with their creators. The first-time visitor may have some mental adjustments to make. Startling colour combinations or the profusion of death imagery can disturb, yet the most exciting pieces are often the most 'Mexican' in spirit. A blouse that the wearer has exuberantly embroidered for her own use with angels and prancing horses holds more long-term interest than a rug woven for the tourist market with the formalized designs of Escher. As this book has tried to show, however, the opportunity to sell to tourists has also inspired some very ingenious and vigorous work.

In Mexico the best examples of popular art are often found in the homes of private collectors. Frida Kahlo's house, which she shared with Diego Rivera until her death, is open to the public; the tiled kitchen, with its array of jugs and pots, is one of the most beautiful in Mexico. In addition there are numerous national collections which visitors can study. Museums in Puebla, Oaxaca and other large towns feature local arts and crafts. In the capital, the top floor of the Museo Nacional de Antropología is given over entirely to the material culture of contemporary Indian peoples. Temporary exhibitions at the Museo Nacional de Culturas Populares often include craftwork, while fine examples of popular art are permanently shown at the Museo Nacional de Artes e Industrias Populares. This organization belongs to the Instituto Nacional Indigenista, as do a number of small regional museums which exist to promote traditional skills.

After seeing good craft examples, it becomes easier to tell the difference between lacquer and paint, or to distinguish a fine weave from a loose one. Working in their different fields many Mexican artisans achieve a delicacy and a refinement rarely surpassed in other countries. It would be a mistake, however, to judge work solely by its technical merits. Visitors from Japan, where the emphasis is on formal perfection, are occasionally surprised by the apparently careless approach shown by some craftworkers. If an embroideress runs out of pink thread in the middle of a petal, she may simply continue in purple if that is what she has to hand. What is to be admired in such instances is the vitality or originality of work.

It is possible to buy splendid examples of Mexican popular art without even leaving the capital. The Museo Nacional de Artes e Industrias Populares, mentioned earlier for its important collection, sells only the finest specimens of traditional crafts. The shop Victor, founded many decades ago by Victor Fosado, is regularly visited by collectors and museum curators from all over the world. In recent years standards have been less well maintained in the shops of FONART, the government crafts agency, but it is hoped that new policies will bring an improvement in the 1990s. Lovers of the Mexican miniature should not fail to visit the diminutive Casa de la Miniatura, where every inch is packed with tiny objects for children and adults.

Most guidebooks recommend shopping in Mexico City's many craftmarkets. In the Ciudadela one can occasionally see crafts such as glass-blowing, or buy beadwork from the Huichol families who settle here periodically. Stall-holders in the Mercado de Londres sometimes stock reasonably good bark paintings and embroideries, while visitors to San Angel often enjoy a trip to the Bazar Sabado, or Saturday bazaar. With few exceptions, however, these different venues do not sell popular art. They offer souvenirs and gifts of varying quality which are dismissed by serious Mexican collectors as 'Mexican curios' – or even 'Mexican curious'.

It is generally more rewarding to visit the markets used by local people. Few places in the capital hold more interest than the Mercado de Sonora. Here closely packed aisles lead past *piñatas*, toys, herbal and magic remedies, pottery and caged birds. The passing of the seasons is reflected: Easter and the Day of the Dead bring Judas figures and skeletons in profusion. Outside the nearby Mercado de la Merced, the approach of Christmas is heralded by painted nativity figures which are sold from dozens of makeshift stalls. Visitors to this area are warned to carry as few valuables as possible.

Outside Mexico City splendid craft objects can be bought in town and country markets. Should guidebooks fail to indicate the chief market day in a given place, this information can be obtained by telephoning the *Presidencia*, or seat of local government. The choice of merchandise is always greatest before a festival. In Michoacán, for example, the huge fair which is held each year before the Day of the Dead in Huancito is attended by potters and toy-makers from Ocumicho and other Purépecha villages. Toluca in the State of Mexico also affords an amazing sight as the Day of the Dead approaches: displayed on tables in the portals of the town centre are thousands of sugar skulls and brightly coloured marzipan figures. Tepalcingo in Morelos is the scene of an immense fair; pottery, baskets, toys and lacquerware from Guerrero and adjoining states are sold here in abundance on the third Friday in Lent.

At fairs and local markets merchandise is sold not just by intermediaries but also by the makers. Purchasers can then discuss production methods and find out where items are from. In shops and craftmarkets which cater to tourists such information is rarely available; if provided, it can often be wrong and should be double-checked elsewhere. In guidebooks tourists are invariably advised to haggle and argue over prices. Sometimes this advice is carried to absurd extremes, however. Prices may be offered which barely cover the cost of materials, and the long-term result will be shoddier work with artisans trying to cut corners still further.

Economic pressures are driving many craftworkers to seek a wider market. Lacquer-workers and wood-carvers from Guerrero and embroiderers from San Pablito, Puebla, arrive in increasing numbers each weekend to sell their wares in the market of Tepoztlán in Morelos. Many artisans offer their work on the streets of Mexico City outside museums and subway stations or beneath the portals of the Zócalo (main square). Some also take their wares to the Lagunilla market, where formerly only antiques and bric-à-brac could be found.

Keen travellers may prefer, however, to visit the distant villages and towns where so much fine work is done, and to see craft objects in their own surroundings. Most craftworkers welcome visitors, and will demonstrate their techniques with generosity and patience. Some places, like Teotitlán del Valle in Oaxaca, have become tourist attractions. Visitors are encouraged to enter workshops where *sarapes* are woven in vast quantities on treadle looms; finished examples are exhibited for sale in every available space. Many potters in Metepec, in the State of Mexico, decorate their homes with clay suns and angels in the hope of attracting potential purchasers. Ocumicho, although hard to reach, receives a surprising number of visitors each year. In the gloom of windowless rooms, fantastical and brightly painted pottery figures line the walls.

Countless small villages, by contrast, receive virtually no visitors. Journeys may be difficult, but on arrival it can prove surprisingly easy to find specialist craftworkers. If one has a name, given in a local market or noted from a book, so much the better. With no such information, one can make enquiries in the main shop and at the *Presidencia*, or stop passers-by to ask the whereabouts of weavers and mask-makers. Language may present a problem: in predominantly Indian areas such as highland Chiapas, Spanish is spoken by relatively few people. But even with basic vocabulary and sign language much can be achieved. Sometimes artisans have finished pieces for sale. If not, they will occasionally agree to sell used objects such as clothing. Many craftworkers only work sporadically when other tasks permit, and a weaver who has to clothe her family may produce only two or three saleable items per year. If makers have nothing to offer, it is worth looking for an intermediary. Most villages have middlemen and middlewomen who buy up the work of their neighbours for re-sale elsewhere. Obviously the cost will be proportionately higher.

Should time permit, work can be commissioned directly from the artisan. It is usual to leave an advance to cover the cost of materials. At this stage both parties must reach a firm agreement as to price, thereby avoiding unpleasant future surprises. Few things are more enjoyable than watching the creation of the piece one expects to own; by studying the different stages of production, one also realizes the amount of work which apparently simple objects can require. On occasion the results may disappoint. Frequently, however, commissioned pieces are of a quality rarely encountered in shops or markets.

The question of price is a delicate one. Geography is a key factor. Families living within a radius of Mexico City and other large towns are usually obliged to charge more for their work than craftworkers in distant villages where the cost of living is lower. Some types of craft are generally cheaper than others regardless of region. Functional pottery remains inexpensive – disproportionately so, in some instances, given the amount of work involved. The cost of materials is decisive. Clay, usually obtained locally, may not represent a significant financial outlay. Textiles, by contrast, are often costly to produce. When purchasers express surprise at apparently high prices, they may be told with good reason that wool is scarce, or that the cost of embroidery thread has doubled. When work is commissioned, an artisan may well find that he has underestimated the cost of materials and that inflation has driven up the price of paint or cloth.

In remote regions where craftworkers rarely sell to outsiders, prices may be unrealistically low. In some instances, however, visitors are surprised to find that an object may actually cost less in a craft shop in town than it does in the maker's house some distance away. It is true that craftworkers are occasionally tempted to charge what they imagine their prosperous-looking visitors can afford, yet it should also be said that many shop and stall owners exploit the poverty of craftworkers. By buying in bulk and even providing materials in advance, they are able to buy work at absurdly low prices. Sometimes visitors undervalue the skills involved. Purchasers who would never quibble over gallery prices for 'works of art' are often loath to pay the charges of craftworkers. Tiburcio Soteno of Metepec recalls an altercation with a Mexican buyer, who commissioned a set of painted pottery animals. Although happy at the outset with the agreed price, the buyer later expressed dissatisfaction when he watched his pieces being modelled. 'Now that I see how quickly and deftly you work, I would like to pay you less', said the visitor. Understandably the potter refused, arguing that it had taken him twenty years of hard work to develop his skill.

The field of Mexican crafts is so broad that it is possible to start a good collection whatever one's financial constraints. At the end of 1989 a one-metre-high tree of life cost approximately one million pesos (equivalent to 250 pounds sterling or 400 US dollars) if ordered directly in Metepec. Superb textiles of museum quality from Sna Jolobil, the Chiapas weavers' association, are frequently priced at over 100 pounds (or 160 US dollars). At the other end of the spectrum, however, it is still possible to buy finely decorated pots and dishes, ingenious folk toys and innumerable other objects for paltry sums.

Wooden masks are popular with many visitors, and the range of styles is immense. Collectors in search of genuine dance masks should proceed with caution, however. Festival masks, which have been worn or might conceivably be worn, come in many guises. Some are finely carved and lacquered, while others may be roughly hewn and painted with industrial gloss paint, yet they are all vigorous creations which will be of lasting interest to ethnographers. Drawing on existing traditions, however, wood-carvers from Guerrero and other states now make increasing numbers of decorative masks for the tourist market. Sometimes these are replicas of actual masks; often they are exotic inventions which show imagination but bear no relation to real dances. Some even have a patina to suggest great age. If asked to part with large sums, visitors are advised to seek a second opinion.

The cost of precious metals continues to rise in Mexico. High-quality gold jewelry can still be bought in Oaxaca city and at La Bola de Oro in Papantla, Veracruz. Most metalsmiths confine themselves to silver, however. Jewelry that is sold in cities is usually stamped; this is rarely the case in country areas, although the metal may be no less pure. In other instances the complexity of the workmanship can outweigh the use of adulterated metals. Visitors should be aware, however, that some jewelry displayed in cities is alpaca, not pure silver, and that cheap stones are often dyed to simulate turquoise, jade and other more costly substances.

Many craft objects are extremely fragile, and thought should be given to packing methods. In outlying areas it is useful to carry sheets of bubble plastic. Pottery that is fired at low temperatures, as in Ocumicho, is apt to break. When buying clay water-jars local women tap them with their knuckles: a clear sound is positive, but a muffled one suggests a hidden crack. For transportation hollows should be padded out; extremities and projecting decorations can be swathed in basic toilet paper. Even the most fragile of sugar figures, if kept dry and carefully wrapped, can be carried long distances. Textiles should always be washed by hand in cold water, yet even under these conditions colours may run. It is sensible, therefore, to test-wash a small corner before immersing the whole. Lacquered objects, if they are to be displayed, can be protected with a coat of wax polish.

In the short term there is little to be gained financially by collecting contemporary Mexican crafts. Nineteenth-century masks and *sarapes* may occasionally fetch high prices in salerooms, but the purchase of modern examples is described by Sotheby's and other London auction houses as 'negative investment'. Much popular art actually decreases in value once it leaves Mexico. It is best, therefore, to buy pieces because one likes and enjoys them.

In my experience one only regrets what one doesn't buy – never what one does. Sometimes collectors pass up a piece that they particularly like, because the price seems high or because the moment is inconvenient; they may hope to find a similar piece in the future, yet never do so. Mexican crafts are rich precisely because no two pieces are ever really identical. In truth there are no rules for collecting. Fine pieces can turn up in the most unlikely places. I bought the embroidered cloth in plate 39 from a pavement seller outside the Cathedral in Mexico City during the Feast of Corpus Christi. It remains one of my favourite pieces, but will not please everybody. Taste is a subjective matter; fortunately the range in Mexico is so vast that a thousand visitors would form a thousand different craft collections – something few countries in the world today could offer.

Obviously shops and galleries outside Mexico cannot hope to offer such an extensive choice, but proximity means that shoppers in the south-west USA are better served than those who live further north or in Europe. Antique Mexican furniture, religious carvings, paintings and early twentieth-century jewelry have been highly valued for some time. In the late 1980s, however, renewed regard for local crafts and contemporary folk art served to reinforce appreciation for Latin-American skills. There is no shortage of shops and galleries specializing in Mexico. In Los Angeles, Solo lo Mejor, Y-Qué, La Luz de Jesus and Sonrisa carry a broad selection of Mexican wares; so too do the None Such Gallery of Santa Monica and The Folk Tree of Pasadena. In Albuquerque Mexican crafts are sold at Casa Talavera and La Planta, while Foreign Traders in Santa Fé offers the work of celebrated folk artists such as Herón Martínez.

Mexican crafts are no longer restricted to the south-west, however. In Philadelphia and Washington, DC, they are sold at The Eyes Gallery and The Phoenix respectively. In and around New York, where there is currently a fashion for south-western styles, many homes and offices now display rugs, wall-hangings and pots. Shops which stock south-western crafts often sell similar items from Mexico, but it is not always considered important to distinguish the place of origin. It should also be said that craftspeople in Mexico are occasionally asked to produce work that could pass as North-American. During the 1980s several treadle-loom weavers in Teotitlán del Valle, Oaxaca, were issued with Navajo pattern books for rugs, and asked to copy designs for the USA. Various shops in New York do, however, sell authentic Mexican crafts. These include Casa Moneo Imports, Sleeping Shadows, Tianguis Folk Art and Mexican Folk Art. In New Jersey, Mexican folk art is sold at Cactus Incorporated. I am grateful to David Velásquez, Jane Weiner, Shay Cunliffe and Susie Symmes for providing information about the sale of Mexican Crafts in the USA.

In England most businesses deal simultaneously in wares from several countries, despite the current vogue for Mexican styles. In 1989 and 1990 several fashion editors promoted the 'Frida Kahlo' look and encouraged a shift from matt-black minimalism to 'South of the Border' colour and exuberance. Liberty of Regent Street mounted a Mexican promotion, and a growing number of small shops now stock limited supplies of Mexican trinkets and fashion accessories. In London, good pottery and glassware is sold by Tapatl. Tumi, which also has branches in Oxford and Bath, specializes in South American crafts but increasingly stocks Mexican jewelry and other items, while large pots, papier mâché figures and iron furniture are available from Montezumas. As its name suggests, the Santa Fé Trading Post concentrates chiefly on styles from the North-American south-west. Although Ends of the Earth has no shop, finely crafted glazed jugs, burnished black pots, *sarapes*, *rebozos* and brocaded weavings are available by mail order. On the whole, however, Mexican imports to England offer little more than a glimpse at the many facets of popular art so abundantly displayed in Mexico or even the USA. All too often fine workmanship is lacking, while high freight costs prohibit the sale of large or fragile pieces. Serious collectors are advised, therefore, to make their own selection in Mexico itself, where objects can be enjoyed in their original context.

List of places mentioned above:

Mexico

Arte Popular en Miniatura, Hamburgo 130, Zona Rosa, Mexico City
Bazar Sabado, Plaza San Jacinto, San Angel, Mexico City
La Bola de Oro, Juárez 200, Papantla, Veracruz
FONART (Fondo Nacional para el Fomento de las Artesanias): main shop and offices, Av. Patriotismo 691, Mexico City 19; branches at Juárez 89, and other sites
Mercado de la Ciudadela, Plaza de la Ciudadela, Mexico City
Mercado de la Lagunilla, Allende and Ecuador, Mexico City
Mercado de la Merced, Anillo de Circunvalación, Mexico City
Mercado de Londres, Londres, Zona Rosa, Mexico City
Mercado de Sonora, Fray Servando T. de Mier (near intersection with Anillo de Circunvalación), Mexico City
Museo Frida Kahlo, Londres 247, Coyoacán, Mexico City
Museo Nacional de Antropología, Paseo de la Reforma (Bosque de Chapultepec), Mexico City
Museo Nacional de Artes e Industrias Populares del INI, Avenida Juárez 44, Mexico City
Museo Nacional de Culturas Populares, Hidalgo 289, Coyoacán, Mexico City
Sna Jolobil, Ex-convento de Santo Domingo, San Cristóbal de las Casas, Chiapas
Victor: Artes Populares Mexicanas, Madero 10-305, Mexico City 1
Victor: Artes Regionales, Porfirio Díaz 111, Oaxaca city

USA

Cactus Incorporated, 21 East Northfield, Livingston, New Jersey 07030
Casa Moneo Imports, 210 W. 14th Street, New York, NY 10011
Casa Talavera, 621 Rio Grande Boulevard, North West Albuquerque, New Mexico 87104
The Eyes Gallery, 402 South Street, Philadelphia, PA 19147
The Folk Tree, 217 S. Fair Oaks Avenue, Pasadena, CA 91105
Foreign Traders, 202 Galisteo Street, Santa Fé, New Mexico 87501
La Luz de Jesus, 7400 Melrose Avenue, Los Angeles, CA 90046
Mexican Folk Art, 108 W. Houston, New York, NY 10012
None Such Gallery, 1211 Montana Avenue, Santa Monica, CA 90403
The Phoenix, 1514 Wisconsin Avenue, North West Washington, DC
La Planta, 3009 Central, North East Albuquerque, New Mexico 87106
Sleeping Shadows, 215 West 10th Street, New York, NY 10014
Solo lo Mejor, 8342 Melrose Avenue, Los Angeles, CA 90069
Sonrisa, 8214 Melrose Avenue, Los Angeles, CA 90046
Tianguis Folk Art, 284 Columbus Avenue, New York, NY 10023
Y-Qué, 4319 Melrose Avenue, Los Angeles, CA 90026

England

Ends of the Earth (mail order only), PO Box 31, Hampton, Middlesex, TW12 2NW
Liberty, Regent Street, London W1
Montezumas, 9 Oak Road, Ealing Broadway, London W5
Santa Fé Trading Post, 34 Bruton Place, London W1
Tapatl, 659 Fulham Road, London SW6
Tumi, 23 Chalk Farm Road, Camden Town, London NW1; New Bond Street Place, Bath, Avon; Little Clarendon Street, Oxford

UNITED STATES OF AMERICA

BAJA CALIFORNIA

BAJA CALIFORNIA SUR

SONORA

CHIHUAHUA

COAHUILA

NUEVO LEÓN

TAMAULIPAS

SINALOA

DURANGO

ZACATECAS

SAN LUIS POTOSÍ

AGS.

NAYARIT

GUANAJUATO

QRO.

HIDALGO

MÉXICO

TAX.

Mexico City D.F.

MOR.

PUEBLA

V E R A C R U Z

GULF

OF

MEXICO

PACIFIC

OCEAN

JALISCO

COLIMA

MICHOACÁN

GUERRERO

Oaxaca

OAXACA

TABASCO

Tuxtla Gutiérrez

CHIAPAS

YUCATÁN

QUINTANA ROO

CAMPECHE

BELIZE

GUATEMALA

N

0   240 Mis
0   360 Km

AGS.   AGUASCALIENTES
MOR.   MORELIA
QRO.   QUERÉTARO
TAX.   TLAXCALA

MEXICO'S INDIGENOUS PEOPLES

It is hard to calculate the Indian population of Mexico. Although various criteria are used to decide who should count as 'Indian', it is usual to equate 'Indianness' with the ability to speak an Indian language. According to the system of classification established by Maurice Swadesh, fifty-three Indian languages are currently spoken in Mexico. Most of these are mutually unintelligible. Many languages are also subdivided into dialects. The figures given below were recorded in the National Census of 1980; numbers are now reckoned to be substantially higher.

The following Indian language-groups are mentioned in this book:

AMUZGO: 18,373 speakers. The Amuzgo are a predominantly agricultural people who reside in twelve communities in adjoining areas of Guerrero and Oaxaca. Before planting, rituals are held. Amuzgo women are fine weavers; many still wear cotton *huipiles* with brocaded designs.

CHATINO: 20,381 speakers. Members of this agricultural group live in the south-west of Oaxaca. Despite cultural similarities with the southern Zapotec and, to a lesser degree, with the lowland Mixtec, the Chatino retain a strong sense of their own identity. There have been several Chatino uprisings since Colonial times.

CHINANTEC: 66,811 speakers. In north-western Oaxaca, where the Chinantec live, the land is fertile and watered by several main rivers. Since 1947 a government programme to develop the Papaloapan Basin has resulted in rapid changes in the region. Chinantec women in conservative communities have retained their traditional clothing styles, however.

CHONTAL (TABASCO): 28,344 speakers. Members of this group belong to the Maya family and inhabit coastal Tabasco. Maize-based foods provide staple nourishment, together with beans, chilli peppers and squash. Until a few years ago the Chontal wore traditional clothing; now, however, they wear contemporary urban styles.

CORA: 11,518 speakers. Closely related to the Huichol, the Cora live in the mountains of the Sierra Madre in northern Nayarit. Crops include maize, beans and squash. Catholicism has fused with native beliefs; of the various festivals celebrated by the Cora, one of the most important is Holy Week. Ceremonies are supervised by shamans.

HUASTEC: 100,467 speakers. The region known as La Huasteca comprises parts of Veracruz, San Luis Potosí, Hidalgo and Tamaulipas. The area inhabited by the Huastec was dramatically reduced after the Conquest, however. Although they belong to the Maya family, the Huastec are geographically distant from other related groups. Crafts are rarely a full-time occupation.

HUAVE: 9826 speakers. Members of this group from Oaxaca live by salt-water lagoons on the Pacific coast. Fishing and agriculture are important activities; women also supplement the family income by weaving. Catholic and native religious elements have fused; many Huave are currently experiencing Baptist evangelization.

HUICHOL: 49,519 speakers. Members of this agricultural group live high up in the Sierra Madre, where the states of Jalisco and Nayarit meet. The Huichol have proved more resistant to outside pressures than most other Mexican groups. Religious beliefs and ceremonies owe little to Christianity.

LACANDÓN: 300 speakers. Deep in the Chiapas rainforest live the Lacandón, who call themselves the *hach winik*, or 'true people'. Under the leadership of Old Chan K'in, members of the northern group at Lake Najá have resisted religious pressure from outside; beliefs and practices are inherited from the ancient Maya. The southern Lacandón, based at Lacanjá, have recently been converted to Christianity by the Summer Institute of Linguistics, while members of a third group at Lake Mensäbäk are now Seventh-Day Adventists.

MAYA (YUCATEC): 630,008 speakers. The ancient Maya were never a single, unified nation; their civilization seems to have been based instead on a loose federation of city states. Although the Maya family today includes a number of peoples in Mexico and other countries, the term is specifically applied to the people of the Yucatán Peninsula. Women from the states of Quintana Roo, Campeche and Yucatán wear distinctive clothing. In conservative communities native beliefs and practices underlie Catholicism.

MAYO: 55,478 speakers. The Mayo live in southern Sonora and northern Sinaloa, and depend upon agriculture for their survival. Their villages are surrounded by *mestizo* communities. Although the Mayo now dress like their non-Indian neighbours, they retain a strong sense of their own identity. This is expressed during Holy Week and other festivals.

MAZAHUA: 181,002 speakers. Members of this group, who belong to the Otomí family, live in the State of Mexico and in adjoining areas of Michoacán; large numbers of Mazahua also subsist in Mexico City. Predominantly an agricultural people, the Mazahua also practise various crafts such as weaving and embroidery.

MAZATEC: 113,523 speakers. Members of this agricultural group live in north-eastern Oaxaca; the construction of a hydro-electric dam in 1954 forced many families to move to southern Veracruz. Although nominal Catholics, the Mazatec retain a belief in native healers. In recent years Mazatec use of hallucinogenic mushrooms near Huautla de Jiménez has attracted considerable outside interest.

MIXE: 69,476 speakers. In the mountainous north-east of Oaxaca, where the Mixe live, peaks rise to over 3000 m. A shortage of agricultural land contributes to Mixe poverty. Although the Mixe are nominal Catholics, they retain a belief in maize spirits and other deities. Reserved in personality, the Mixe are wary of outsiders.

MIXTEC: 281,622 speakers. The Mixtec are an agricultural people who live in northern and western Oaxaca; they also inhabit adjoining areas of Guerrero and Puebla. The region known as La Mixteca is divided into highland, lowland and coastal zones. Before the Conquest the Mixtec excelled as builders, goldsmiths and codex-painters. Today their descendants wear traditional clothing and practise a wide number of crafts. The TACUATE are a sub-group.

NAHUA: 1,317,001 speakers. Náhuatl-speaking peoples constitute Mexico's largest indigenous group. Although they live chiefly in Puebla, Veracruz, Hidalgo, Guerrero, San Luis Potosí, Tlaxcala, Morelos, the State of Mexico and the Federal District, there are smaller groups in Oaxaca, Jalisco, Michoacán, Nayarit and Tabasco. The Nahua speak the ancient Aztec language, with minor dialect differences, and retain many ancient craft skills such as weaving.

NORTHERN TEPEHUAN: 2289 speakers. Members of this isolated and scattered group inhabit the mountains of south-western Chihuahua. A subsistence diet is provided through agriculture and hunting. Although nominal Catholics, the Northern Tepehuan retain their belief in a series of spirit beings.

OTOMÍ: 279,762 speakers. One of the largest Indian groups in Mexico, the Otomí live chiefly in the State of Mexico and in central Hidalgo; they also inhabit small areas of Puebla, Veracruz, Querétaro, Michoacán, Tlaxcala, Guanajuato and Morelos. Their way of life varies according to geography and climate. Although the Otomí are nominal Catholics, a number of indigenous beliefs have been retained in villages such as San Pablito.

PURÉPECHA: 92,642 speakers. The Purépecha, or Tarascan Indians, live in the north of Michoacán. Agricultural production includes maize, beans and squash; fishing and the sale of forest-wood provide additional income, as do crafts such as wood-carving, basketry, pottery-making, weaving and embroidery.

SERI: 400 speakers. A nomadic group before the Conquest, the Seri maintained an independent existence well into the twentieth century. Today they are settled at Punta Chueca and Desemboque on the desert coast of Sonora, and on Tiburón Island. They live by fishing, and supplement their income through wood-carving and basketry. Post-Conquest attempts at conversion by Catholic missionaries were unsuccessful; since the 1950s, however, many Seri have embraced the Protestant faith.

TARAHUMARA: 57,118 speakers. The Tarahumara remain one of the least acculturated groups in the Americas. In their own language they call themselves *rarámuri*, literally runners-on-foot. There is a shortage of agricultural land in the mountains of south-western Chihuahua where the Tarahumara live, and conditions are harsh. Events from the Catholic calendar are celebrated in a syncretic fashion, together with native festivals.

TEPEHUA: 8043 speakers. Closely related to the Totonac, the Tepehua live in northern Veracruz and north-eastern Hidalgo; in recent years they have also settled a small area of Puebla. Those with access to land depend on agriculture for their survival; others hire themselves out as labourers. Crafts such as pottery and basketry are for home consumption.

TOJOLABAL: 22,222 speakers. The Tojolabal, who belong to the Maya family, live on agricultural land in south-eastern Chiapas near the border with Guatemala. Many people keep pigs, turkeys or chickens. Men earn additional income by working on neighbouring coffee plantations.

TOTONAC: 185,836 speakers. Before the Conquest the lands of the Totonac were known as Totonacapan; today their descendants live in south-eastern Veracruz and northern Puebla. Mountain areas are cool and misty, coastal zones hot and humid. Extensive deforestation, cattle ranching and the search for oil have disrupted traditional agriculture in the Papantla region. The Totonac have retained a large number of dances; these are now performed during Catholic festivals.

TRIQUE: 7974 speakers. Grouped into five communities and smaller settlements, the Trique inhabit eastern Oaxaca; their lands, high up in the Sierra Madre mountains, are misty and often cold. Many Trique women wear handsome home-woven clothing. Although there are cultural variations among Trique villages, none are as great as that between the Trique and their neighbours, the Mixtec.

TZELTAL: 212,520 speakers. This group, which belongs to the Maya family, lives in central Chiapas. Agriculture, which is central to life, requires various rituals. Native and Catholic elements have fused, and costly *fiestas* are celebrated in honour of the saints. Men and women in several communities wear traditional clothing, often woven on the backstrap loom.

TZOTZIL: 131,825 speakers. In Mexico the Tzotzil ('the people of the bat') are outnumbered only by the Yucatec Maya as speakers of a Maya language. They inhabit highland areas of central Chiapas, and adhere with unusual tenacity to their cultural traditions. Like their neighbours, the Tzeltal, they are excellent weavers. The dead are buried with their personal belongings.

ZAPOTEC: 347,006 speakers. Members of this important linguistic group live in Oaxaca; their language is subdivided into a number of dialects, which are often mutually unintelligible. Before the Conquest the Zapotec excelled as builders and ceramists. Today, fine pots and treadle-loomed *sarapes* are made in the Valley of Oaxaca, while women from the Isthmus of Tehuantepec are famed for their flamboyant clothing and skill as traders.

GLOSSARY

appliqué   Technique whereby shaped sections of cloth are stitched to a cloth background.

batik   Method for resist-dyeing cloth: designs are created by applying a waxy substance to selected areas, rendering them impervious to dye.

charro   In Spain the term once denoted a peasant from the province of Salamanca, but in Mexico it is applied to horsemen; modern-day charros retain a showy style of dress.

conquistadores   Term applied to the Spanish Conquerors led by Hernán Cortés.

costumbrista   Concerned with customs and manners; this term is often applied to novels and paintings of the nineteenth century.

fiesta   Festival, party.

genre figurine   Figurine depicting social types.

huipil   Woman's sleeveless tunic of pre-Conquest origin (from the Náhuatl huipilli).

ikat   This technique takes its name from the Indonesian word mengikat, which means to tie. Method used by dyers to pattern yarn before it is woven.

machete   Big knife, often used for agricultural tasks.

maguey   Popular term for the Mexican agave, which includes some two hundred species.

mariachi   Musician belonging to itinerant orchestra; originally from Guadalajara, mariachi musicians now perform in most places and wear flamboyant costumes.

Mesoamerica   Middle America: generally defined as a cultural area extending from Sinaloa and the Pánuco River along Mexico's Pacific coast down to north-west Costa Rica, and from present-day Tampico in Tamaulipas along Mexico's Gulf coast into Honduras.

mestizo   Mexican of mixed European and Indian descent.

milagro   Literally, miracle; by extension the term is applied to ex-votos, which are offered to the saints after a miraculous cure or rescue.

nacimiento   Nativity scene.

netting   Technique whereby rows of pliable yarn are knotted or looped into the preceding row to create open-meshed fabric.

papier mâché   Material consisting of paper-pulp or sheets of paper pasted together.

peyote   Hallucinatory cactus (Lophorora Williamsii).

pointillisme   French term for the use of separate dots of pure colour in painting.

pulque   Mildly alcoholic drink made by fermenting the sweet sap (aguamiel, literally, 'honey water') of Agave atrovirens and other agave species.

quechquemitl   Woman's cape-like shoulder-garment of pre-Conquest origin.

rebozo   Rectangular shawl.

retablo   Reredos, or altarpiece. Also picture that gives thanks in pictorial form for divine intervention.

sarape   Blanket, often with an opening for the head.

servilleta   Cloth, often used for ceremonial purposes or to cover food.

tortilla   Flat cake of unleavened corn meal.

twining   Technique used for textiles and basketry whereby two or more weft elements are twisted around each other to enclose two or more warp elements.

BIBLIOGRAPHY

Altamirano, Ignacio Manuel et al., *Títeres: La compañía de titeres de Roseta Aranda*, Mexico 1989

Anawalt, Patricia Rieff, *Indian Clothing before Cortés: Mesoamerican Costumes from the Codices*, Norman 1981

Barba de Piña Chan, Beatriz and Marita Martínez del Rio de Redo, 'Alhajas mexicanas', *Artes de México* XX, 165, Mexico City 1974

Barrera Vazquez, Alfredo et al., 'Mitos, ritos y hechicerias', *Artes de México* XVI, 124, Mexico City 1969

Becerril Straffon, Rodolfo, *Los artesanos nos dijeron*, Mexico City 1981

Beltrán, Alberto, *La pintura popular de México*, Mexico City 1982

Benson Gyles, Anna and Chloë Sayer, *Of Gods and Men: Mexico and the Mexican Indian*, London 1980

Brody Esser, Janet, *Faces of Fiesta: Mexican Masks in Context* (exhib. cat.), San Diego 1981
— *Behind the Mask in Mexico*, Santa Fé, New Mexico 1988

Calderon de la Barca, Frances, *Life in Mexico*, London 1843

Carrillo Azpeitia, Rafael et al., *Lo efímero y eterno del arte popular mexicano* (2 vols), Mexico City 1971

Castelló Yturbide, Teresa et al., 'El juguete mexicano', *Artes de México* XVI, 125, Mexico City 1969
— 'El rebozo', *Artes de México* XVIII, 142, Mexico City 1971
— 'El maque: Lacas de Michoacán, Guerrero y Chiapas', *Artes de México* XIX, 153, Mexico City 1972

Codex Florentino, see Sahagún, Fray Bernardino

Codex Mendoza, fac. edn, 3 vols, London 1938
Codex Zouche, fac. edn, New York 1975

Coe, Michael D., *Mexico* (revised edn), London and New York 1984

Cordry, Donald B., *Mexican Masks*, Austin 1980

Cordry, Donald B. and Dorothy M., *Mexican Indian Costumes*, Austin 1968

Cortés, Hernán, *Hernán Cortés: Letters from Mexico*, trans. A.R. Pagden (ed.), New York 1971

Cortina, Leonor, Velázquez Thierry, Luz de Lourdes et al., 'La Talavera de Puebla', *Artes de México* nueva época, 3, Mexico City 1989

Covarrubias, Miguel, *Mexico South: The Isthmus of Tehuantepec*, New York 1946

Davis, Mary L. and Greta Pack, *Mexican Jewelry*, Austin 1963

Díaz del Castillo, Bernal, *The True History of the Conquest of New Spain*, 5 vols, intro. and trans. by A.P. Maudslay, London 1908–16

Díaz de Cossio, Alberto and Francisco Javier Álvarez, *La cerámica colonial y contemporánea*, Mexico City 1982

Dirección General de Culturas Populares, *Índice Bibliográfico sobre artesanías*, Mexico City 1988

Durán, Fray Diego, *Book of the gods and rites and The ancient calendar*, trans. Fernando Horcasitas and Doris Heyden (eds), Norman 1971

Enciso, Jorge, *Design Motifs of Ancient Mexico*, New York 1953
— *Designs from Pre-Columbian Mexico*, New York 1971

Espejel, Carlos, *Las artesanias tradicionales en México*, Mexico City 1972
— *Las jicaras de Acapetlahuaya*, Mexico City 1973
— *Céramica popular mexicana*, Mexico City and Barcelona 1975

— *Olinalá*, Mexico City 1976
— *Mexican Folk Crafts*, Barcelona 1978
— *Juguetes mexicanos*, Mexico City 1981
— *Guia artesanal del Estado de México*, Toluca 1984

Fernández Ledesdma, Gabriel, *Juguetes mexicanos*, Mexico City 1930

Field, Frederick, *Pre-Hispanic Mexican Stamp Designs*, New York 1974

Francis, Peter, Jr, 'Jade Beads and the Conquest of Mexico', *Lapidary Journal USA*, January 1985

Furst, Peter and Salomón Nahmad, *Nitos y artes huicholes*, Mexico City 1972

Gage, Thomas, *Thomas Gage's Travels in the New World*, J.E.S. Thompson (ed.), Norman 1969

Giffords, Gloria Kay, *Mexican Folk Retablos: Masterpieces on Tin*, Tucson 1974

Guiteras-Holmes, Calixta, *Perils of the Soul: The World View of a Tzotzil Indian*, New York 1961

Gutiérrez, Tonatiúh and Elektra L. Mompradé, 'El arte popular de México', *Artes de México* numero extraordinario, Mexico City 1970–71
— 'Danzas y bailes populares', *Historia General del Arte Mexicano*, Editorial Hermes, Mexico City 1976

Guzmán Contreras, Alejandro, *Artesanos de la Sierra Norte de Puebla*, Mexico City 1977
— *Las lacas*, Mexico City 1982

Harvey, Marian, *Crafts of Mexico*, New York 1973
— *Mexican Crafts and Craftspeople*, Philadelphia 1986

Herández, Francisco Javier, 'El juguete popular en México', *Enciclopedia Mexicana del Arte*, 10, Mexico City 1950

Heter, James, and Juelke, Paula Marie, *The Saltillo Sarape* (exhib. cat.), Santa Barbara 1978

Johnson, Irmgard Weitlaner, *Design Motifs on Mexican Indian Textiles* (2 vols), Graz 1976

Landa, Fray Diego de, *Relación de las cosas de Yucanán*, trans. and annot. Alfred M. Tozzer, Cambridge, MA 1941

Lechuga, Ruth D., *El traje indigena de México: su evolución desde la época prehispánica hasta la actualidad*, Mexico City 1982

Léon-Portilla, Miguel, *The Broken Spears: The Aztec account of the conquest of Mexico*, trans. Lysander Kemp, London 1962

Lumholtz, Carl, 'Symbolism of the Huichol Indians', *Memoirs of the American Museum of Natural History 3*, Anthropology 2 (I): 1–228, New York 1900

— *Unknown Mexico* (2 vols), London 1903

— 'Decorative Art of the Huichol Indians', *Memoirs of the American Museum of Natural History 3*, Anthropology 2 (3): 279–327, New York 1904

Madsen, William, 'The Nahua', in Vogt, Evon Z., *Handbook of Middle American Indians* (see below)

Mapelli Mozzi, Carlota, and Teresa Castello Yturbide, *El traje indigena en México* (2 vols), Mexico City 1965–68

Marín de Paalen, Isabel, 'Etno-artesanias y arte popular', *Historia General del Arte Mexicano*, Mexico City 1974

Mata Torres, Ramón, 'Vida y Arte de los Huicholes' (2 vols), *Artes de México* XIX, 160, 161, Mexico City 1972

Matos Moctezuma, Eduardo, 'Miccaihuitl: El Culto a la Muerte', *Artes de México* XVIII, 145, Mexico City 1971

Matos Moctezuma, Eduardo et al., *Lebende Tote: Totenkult in Mexico*, Bremen 1986

Modiano, Nancy, *Indian Education in the Chiapas Highlands*, New York 1973

Monsiváis, Carlos, *El arte de Roberto Ruiz*, Mexico City 1988

Morley, Sylvanus G., *The Ancient Maya* (third edition revised by George W. Brainerd), Stanford, CA 1956

Morris, Walter F., Fr, *A Millennium of Weaving in Chiapas*, Mexico 1984

— *Luchetik: El lenguaje textil de los Altos de Chiapas (The Woven Word from Highland Chiapas)*, Mexico 1986

— *Living Maya*, New York 1987

Motolinía (Fray Toribio de Benavente), *Motolinía's History of the Indians of New Spain*, trans. and annot. by F.B. Steck, Washington 1951

Moya Rubio, Victor José, *Máscaras: la otra cara de México*, Mexico City 1978

Muller, Florencia and Barbara Hopkins, *A Guide to Mexican Ceramics*, Mexico City 1974

Murillo, Gerardo (Dr Atl), *Las artes populares de México*, Mexico 1980

Nebel, Carlos, *Voyage pittoresque et archéologique dans la partie la plus intéressante du Mexique*, Paris 1836

Olivier Vega, Beatriz et al., *The Days of the Dead: a Mexican tradition*, Mexico City 1988

Paz, Octavio, *The Labyrinth of Solitude*, trans. Lysander Kemp, London 1967

Pennington, Campbell W., *The Tarahumar of Mexico*, Salt Lake City, Utah 1963

Pettit, Florence H. and Robert M., *Mexican Folk Toys*, New York 1978

Pomar, Maria Teresa, *Danza-máscara y rito-ceremonia*, Mexico City 1982

— *El Día de los Muertos: The Life of the Dead in Mexican Folk Art* (exhib. cat.), Fort Worth 1987

Posada, José Guadalupe, *José Guadalupe Posada: Ilustrador de la vida mexicana*, Mexico City 1963

— *José Guadalupe Posada: Messenger of Mortality*, London 1989

Reynoso, Louisa, *La cerámica indígena en México*, Mexico City 1982

— *Ocumicho*, Mexico City 1984

Romero de Terreros y Vinent, Manuel, *Las artes industriales en la Nueva España*, Mexico City 1982

Rossbach, Ed, *Baskets as Textile Art*, London 1974

Sackmann, Wolfgang et al., *Wer den Ton Beseelt ... cerámica mexicana: Katalog zur Ausstellung zeitgenössicher mexikanischer Keramik*, Hildesheim 1986

Sahagún, Fray Bernardino de (ed.), *Codex Florentino: General History of the Things of New Spain*, trans. Arthur J.O. Anderson and Charles E. Dibble, Monographs 2–13 (14 parts), Santa Fé 1950–69

Saldívar, Antonio and Abraham Mauricio

Salazar, *El ciclo mágico de los días*, Mexico City 1985

Sandstrom, Alan R. and Pamela Effrein, *Traditional Papermaking and Paper Cult Figures of Mexico*, Norman and London 1986

Sayer, Chloë, *Crafts of Mexico*, London 1977

— *Mexican Costume* (published in the USA as *Costumes of Mexico*), London and Austin 1985

— *Mexican Textile Techniques*, London 1988

Scheffler, Lilian, 'Juegos tradicionales del Estado de Tlaxcala', *Estudios de Folklore y de Arte Popular 3*, Mexico City 1976

— *Juguetes y miniaturas populares de México*, Mexico City 1982

— *Grupos indígenas de México*, Mexico City 1989

Smith, Bradley, *Mexico: A History in Art*, London 1975

Soustelle, Jacques, *Daily Life of the Aztecs on the Eve of the Spanish Conquest*, London 1963

Standley, Paul, *Trees and Shrubs of Mexico*, Washington, DC 1961

Starr, Frederick, *Catalogue of a Collection of Objects Illustrating the Folklore of Mexico*, London 1899

Tax, Sol, Wigberto Jiménez Moreno et al., *Heritage on Conquest, the Ethnology of Middle America*, New York 1952

Thiele, Eva María, *El Maque, estudio histórico sobre un bello arte*, Morelia 1982

Toor, Frances, *A Treasury of Mexican Folkways*, New York 1976

Tylor, Sir Edward B., *Anahuac; or Mexico and the Mexicans, Ancient and Modern*, London 1961

Untract, Oppi, *Jewelry Concepts and Technology*, London 1987

Vaillant, George C., *Artists and Craftsmen in Ancient Central America*, New York 1949

Vexler, Jill, *El textil mexicano: Línea y color* (exhib. cat.), Mexico City 1988

Vogt, Evon Z. et al., *Handbook of Middle American Indians 7–8*, Ethnology (1–2), Austin 1969

Zaldivar, María Luisa Laura, *La cestería en México*, Mexico City 1982

Zingg, Robert Nowry, *The Huichols: Primitive Artists*, New York 1938

INDEX

Acknowledgments

Colour illustrations
References are to plate numbers

The author would like to thank the following for kindly allowing objects from their collections to be photographed:
Robin Bath: *154*
Elizabeth Carmichael: *4, 71, 110, 112*
Josefina Durán: *93*
Celia Lowenstein: *6, 74*
Museum of Mankind, London: *3, 5, 11, 20, 23, 25, 34, 37, 40, 57, 59, 60, 63, 70, 77, 79, 82, 83, 84, 98, 99, 101, 108, 130, 137, 138, 143, 150, 153, 157, 158*
Mab Sayer: *68, 96*

The following artefacts are from the author's own collection:
1, 2, 7, 8, 9, 10, 12–19, 21, 22, 24, 26–31, 33, 38, 39–42, 44, 45, 46, 48–56, 58, 61, 62, 64, 65–67, 69, 72, 73, 75, 76, 78, 80, 81, 85–92, 94, 95, 97, 100, 102, 103, 106, 107, 111, 113–29, 131–36, 139–42, 144–49, 151, 152, 154, 156, 159, 160

Black-and-white photographs and line drawings
References are to page numbers

Photographs
Courtesy of the Trustees of the British Museum: 68
Ruth D. Lechuga: 20, 70, 86, 109, 134
Museo Nacional de Antropología, Mexico City: 18, 50
Marcos Ortiz: 55, 82
Mariana Yampolsky: 2, 6, 8 (top left), 71, 106 (top left)

Line Drawings
Codex Florentino: *General History of the Things of New Spain*, by Fray Bernardino de Sahagún: 21 (top right), 66, 85, 108
Codex Mendoza: 108
Codex Nuttall: 84
Codex Vindobonensis: 23
Codex Zouche: 21 (bottom left), 84
Mary L. Davis, illustration from *Mexican Jewelry*, by Mary L. Davis and Greta Pack (c) 1963: 53, 56. By permission of the University of Texas Press.
Jorge Enciso, *Designs from Pre-Columbian Mexico*, New York 1971: 24, 25; and from *Design Motifs of Ancient Mexico*, New York 1953: 51
Dr Patrick Gallagher, illustration from *Mexico* by Michael D. Coe, London and New York 1984: 67
David Lavender: 26, 83, 106 (right), 107
Carl Lumholtz, *Unknown Mexico* (2 vols), London 1903: 30, 130
Manuel Manilla: 8 (right)
Carlos Merida, illustrations copyright 1947, 1975 by Crown Publishers, Inc. Reprinted from *A Treasury of Mexican Folkways* by Frances Toor, by permission of Crown Publishers, Inc.: 110, 136
Salazar Monroy, *Forja Colonial de Puebla*, Puebla: 54, 88
José Guadalupe Posada: 111
Chloë Sayer: 27, 28, 29, 132, 133
Susan Walker: 19